The College Influence on Student Character

The College Influence on Student Character

An exploratory study in selected colleges and universities made for the Committee for the Study of Character Development in Education

by EDWARD D. EDDY, JR.
assisted by
MARY LOUISE PARKHURST
JAMES S. YAKOVAKIS

AMERICAN COUNCIL ON EDUCATION
Washington, D.C.

PRINTED IN THE UNITED STATES OF AMERICA BY
GEORGE BANTA COMPANY, INC., MENASHA, WISCONSIN

FOREWORD

THE VIRTUAL explosion of scientific discovery during the first half of the twentieth century has propelled our society down the road of material progress at an astonishing rate. Our achievements in learning how to manipulate the forces of nature, however, have all but outdistanced our achievements in learning how to direct the forces now at our disposal. Thus, the hands that control great power must become certain hands.

Actually, the evolution of this condition was perceived a long time ago, for, in a letter from Benjamin Franklin to Joseph Priestley in 1780, there appears this statement: "The rapid progress true science now makes occasions my regretting sometimes that I was born too soon. It is impossible to imagine the height to which may be carried in a thousand years the power of man over matter. . . . Oh, that moral science were in as fair a way of improvement!"

Happily, there is a growing appreciation today of the urgent necessity to develop in oncoming generations the strength of character to match the responsibilities that will be heaped upon the educated leader.

Recognizing a need for an organized attempt to assess influences on character in the college setting, as well as to gather information on what is being tried, what succeeds best, and what limitations exist, a number of interested persons met several years ago under the auspices of the American Council on Education to draw up a study plan. They were encouraged in their efforts by the interest of the Calkins Foundation, which made a generous grant in support of a study.

After a number of suggestions were made, a proposal was written, a committee appointed, and preliminary meetings held. In order to become acquainted with the problem at firsthand, the committee members decided to make individual visits to institutions of their own choice. Following these exploratory visits to twenty-five institutions, the members reconvened to report their findings. They agreed that the success of the study would depend largely on finding a director with wide campus experience, sensitivity to the issues involved, and unusual perceptivity. Fortunately, the Council was able to find such a man in Dr. Edward D. Eddy, Jr., the vice-president and provost of the University of New Hampshire.

This volume is Dr. Eddy's report. The unique method which he chose for gathering his material gives a special emphasis and freshness to the conclusions. His findings are sobering, yet hopeful. If the present state of affairs is disturbing, at least there are clues as to how to improve it. By raising the level of expectancy of both students and faculty members, Dr. Eddy declares, we can achieve cultivation of both mind and value—a dual goal of excellence. Intellect and character, he finds, reinforce one another. Far from being antithetical or contending goals, he says, the two ideally proceed together in higher learning. Wherever one is emphasized and the other slighted, both suffer. When both are conceived to be important elements of higher learning, each prospers.

The Council is grateful not only to the Calkins Foundation for its original interest and support but also to the Ford Foundation for its supplementary grant which made possible the completion of the work. The Council is grateful also to the members of the committee who gave time and thought to the planning of the study and to Dr. Eddy and his assistants, Mr. Yakovakis and Miss Parkhurst, who so ably conducted it. Finally, the Council is indebted to the president and trustees of the University of New Hampshire, who made it possible for Dr. Eddy to take time away from part of his official duties so that he might undertake the study reported here.

The Council confidently hopes and expects that this study will lead to the kind of debate and evaluation from which new and sounder approaches to higher education may emerge.

ARTHUR S. ADAMS, *President*
American Council on Education

November 1958

PREFACE

THE STAFF for this study consisted of three members—a director and two assistants—but many more people throughout the country contributed to whatever value the study may have. The staff is grateful for the cooperation of the colleges and universities included in our visits. The responsible officers in these institutions gave us complete freedom to approach any member of the campus community and assisted in making detailed arrangements in order that we might participate and observe as fully as possible. Their competence and graciousness enabled us to cover a wide territory, both figuratively and geographically, in a fairly short period of time.

In recent years American colleges and universities have been accused of intransigent opposition to criticism and change. From our experience, however, the fact that these institutions were willing to cooperate so fully and to open themselves so completely to scrutiny is strong evidence of their genuine concern for improvement.

We appreciate particularly the substantial assistance and support from the committee for the study as well as from the staff of the American Council on Education, including in particular President Arthur S. Adams and the committee's secretary, Nicholas C. Brown.

A number of others assisted in ways large and small. Among our informal consultants have been David Riesman of the University of Chicago and now of Harvard, Frederick M. Jervis of the University of New Hampshire, W. Max Wise of Columbia University, Martha Peterson of the University of Wisconsin, Dyke Brown of the Ford Foundation, Ordway Tead of Harper and Brothers, Burton P. Fowler of the Fund for the Advancement of Education, and Mervin Freedman of the Mellon Foundation at Vassar College.

Personally I am indebted also to President Eldon L. Johnson and others of my colleagues at the University of New Hampshire who offered helpful suggestions and criticisms. These are but a few of the many who encouraged us in this enterprise but who, naturally, should not and cannot be held responsible for what is said here.

EDWARD D. EDDY, JR.

Durham, New Hampshire
August 1958

CONTENTS

1. Character in the Colleges

THIS REPORT is the result of visits, extending over a period of one year, to twenty American colleges and universities. It is an attempt to describe and delineate character influences and programs as they were reported to us by students and members of the faculty and as we observed them. Because the purpose and the method of the study condition what is reported, we will attempt to describe briefly what we tried to do and how we tried to do it.

The Aim of the Study

Technological advances in the last half century have brought a special responsibility to American colleges and universities. The nation is dependent on them for a ready supply of competently trained men and women. But the task of the colleges[1] is not that simple. To skill must be added wisdom. The colleges are asked to furnish men and women capable of making decisions on which may rest the fate of millions of people throughout the world and capable of leading lives which set a worthy example for all men.

Our study was conceived and carried forth in the hope that we might be able to identify some of the ways by which the colleges can fulfill their obligation to this greater task. Though the contributions of higher education have been substantial, there is reason to feel that the student in pursuit of a degree and the college wrapped in its own day-to-day operation may have failed to capitalize adequately on the great potential in both youth and higher learning. We wanted to explore the relationship between intellectual training and character influence; to determine how

[1] For ease of expression, the term "colleges" will be used in place of "colleges and universities" where reference is made to both types of institutions.

the colleges, their students, and their faculty, approach the task of education; and to observe programs in operation which show signs of effectiveness.

The time and funds available made it impossible to undertake a complete review of character influences and programs. Furthermore, a pilot study seemed more desirable at this stage. We felt that a broad overview might lead to the identification of particular aspects deserving more thorough analysis. We intended this to be a description of the here and now, rather than an evaluation of the end product. Because of the small size of the sampling, the study could not pretend to be a complete survey of conditions in American colleges and universities. Comments and conclusions, therefore, apply only to a majority of the colleges visited and in the context of our method.

A Working Definition of Character

Terminology is troublesome in any study but we found it particularly so in the area of character. Like religion and politics, character means many things to many people, and personal concepts often are guarded jealously. They range from the most religious to the extremely secular. Among some, character is synonymous with morality, but the term "moral" immediately raises questions of meaning. To others, character may include morality and yet be much more. Through most concepts, however, there appears to run a thread of unity. Some degree of consistency of thought and action is considered paramount to effective behavior emanating from character.

At the outset the staff of the study determined that, for its own purposes, an explicit working definition of character was desirable. We sought one which would reflect the potentiality of higher education to affect attitudes and values. The staff agreed, therefore, that character is *intelligent direction and purposeful control of conduct by definite moral principles*. In this sense, character is reflected in the conversion of commitments into consistent application to the complex and varied activities of life. Thus, character is found in action based on principle rather than on that dictated by pressure or expediency. The word "moral" is used to connote excellence in practice or conduct.

In establishing the link between mind and value, Robert Havighurst and Hilda Taba point out:

> Wise control of conduct is possible to the extent that the individual understands why certain acts are desirable and others undesirable; to the extent that he foresees the consequences of his acts; and to the extent that he becomes aware of certain general moral principles, standards, and values and their relationship to conduct; in other words, to the extent that he formulates a rationale for his conduct and guides his behavior accordingly.[2]

Our definition is a behavioral interpretation. We believe that education has little meaning unless it results in constructive use. Character as an intellectual commitment alone is valueless unless it is accompanied by living proof of the commitment. Belief is affirmed in behavior. An important test of the substance of education should lie in the deepest convictions, the actual conduct, and the attitude exhibited in the life of the college graduate.

The Assumptions of the Study

Beyond the working definition, we felt that certain assumptions were necessary before we proceeded further. We agreed, therefore, to three: (1) that among its responsibilities the American college should include a conscious concern for the character of its students; (2) that it is not desirable to separate the training of the intellect from values which impinge on the life and thought of the student; (3) that basic convictions and values are formed in the early years and primarily in the home, but the college can modify convictions and values both for good and for ill. It can assist in turning vague concepts into convictions by the encouragement of conscious examination and evaluation and by

[2] Havighurst and Taba, *Adolescent Character and Personality* (New York: John Wiley & Sons, 1949), p. 12.

the opportunity for positive practice. As the study progressed, these assumptions were modified in relation to what we observed.

The Method of the Study

Essentially we employed the participant-observer approach[3] modified by inclusion of more formal, open-ended interviews with both students and members of the faculty. In this way, our actual observations stemming from participation in the life of a campus were checked and supplemented. Two of the three members of the staff were a young man and woman recently graduated from college. It was their assignment during their visits to the colleges covered in the study to become as much a part of the campus as possible. On each campus they lived with the students in dormitories, fraternities, or sororities, for periods ranging in length from a few days to a total of three weeks, depending on the size of the institution. They ate with students, went to class and to activity meetings with them, and participated in their conversations and late evening discussions. In addition, they interviewed members of the faculty and staff and attended some faculty committee sessions. The daily schedule permitted time for specific follow-up of those individuals and groups most frequently identified through conversations and interviews.

A typical day began about 7 A.M. in a living unit. Breakfast with roommates or students down the hall was followed by attendance at a class or observation of a meeting of personnel deans and officers, followed by more classes, conversations over coffee in the student union, and interviews with faculty. The staff member often lunched with a group of student leaders and then repeated in the afternoon the schedule of the morning. The late afternoon and evening were devoted to participating in student activity groups, student government bodies, or faculty sessions, as well as

[3] For a more detailed description of this method, see William Foote Whyte, "Observational Field-work Methods," in Marie Jahoda, Morton Deutsch, and Stuart W. Cooke, *Research Methods in Social Relations* (New York: Dryden Press, 1951), II, 491–513.

to recording the interview and observational data accumulated during the day. In the late evening the staff member often visited the local coffeehouse or tavern for a snack with his or her newly acquired friends. The discussions back at the dorm or fraternity lasted well into the night.

The director of the study visited a majority of the campuses, although his stay on each was necessarily brief. He talked with administrative officers, faculty members, and some students. This provided a further check on the data and observations gained through the participant observers. In this way, though the time on each campus was limited, we began to feel the pulse of the college student and to understand a bit better his reactions to certain planned and unplanned influences.

In the observations which follow we have leaned heavily upon the reaction of students to their collegiate experience. We believe that how students receive their education conditions what they receive. The idea sometimes expressed that student reactions are immaterial and immature seems to us to dismiss too easily one of the most important sources of suggestions for modification and improvement. Despite their sometime superficiality, perceptive students are capable of analyzing well the experience they undergo. What they do not say may also be as significant as what they do say.

Twenty colleges and universities[4] located in seventeen different states extending from California to New England cooperated in the study. In a study of this type, selection of adequate sample is one of the most difficult problems. From the many possible criteria, we selected the following. We looked for some indication of concern for the general area to be studied. Once having assembled a rather large list of institutions, we narrowed the number down by type, size, and location. In other words, the assumptions of the college were important. Thus, among our final twenty, we included several Protestant colleges, two of the Roman Catholic

[4] See Appendix for a list of the cooperating institutions.

faith, a number of nonsectarian privately controlled institutions, and six of varying size which are supported basically by federal, state, or municipal governments.

The number of undergraduates enrolled in the colleges on our list runs from less than one hundred at Goddard to nearly fourteen thousand at the University of Wisconsin. With the exception of the United States Naval Academy (chosen because of the special emphasis on character in the military establishments), we did not attempt to visit single-purpose institutions such as teachers colleges and technical schools.

For the most part our observations are concerned with the traditional student of the seventeen to twenty-two age range who completes in four consecutive years the requirements for a baccalaureate degree. We have also limited ourselves somewhat to the resident student, although we have included three or four colleges or universities with large commuting populations.

Reactions to and from the Visits

Everywhere we traveled we found the majority of students willing and sometimes anxious to talk about their own educational experiences, about influences upon them, and about their own actions and reactions. In some cases we noted a sense of urgency to discuss the more basic questions of life. It seemed to reveal an aspect of college students not fully appreciated. In addition, the students appeared to us to be perceptive and honest in their acknowledgment of what was good and what was poor in their campus life. Members of the faculty and staff, too, were eager to explore fully in conversation all the ramifications of the questions we put to them. Indeed, their interest sometimes made it difficult for us to keep on schedule and for the staff observers to participate in student life as unobtrusively as possible.

We began our study with the assumption that students on the whole talk more easily to someone of their own age and sex. Our experience, we believe, confirms this assumption. Furthermore, we found that both students and faculty members were inclined to talk more freely and frankly with an outsider. Such a conversation did not run the danger of intruding on the more immediate as well as long-term involvement with the group of which the individual was a part. This reaction was conditioned, quite naturally, by some protectiveness with regard to one's own alma mater, although it was lessened by our assurances of anonymity.

As might be expected, we did encounter a certain pride of privacy in some cases. Other studies have shown this to be a common reaction not just of people in a college setting but in all society. It was surprising, however, to encounter many students who appeared to have had little previous experience with an open discussion of values. Some, for instance, hesitated in conversation and then observed, "You know, I haven't really thought much about that before." As a result, there appeared in some of our interviews a repetition of trite phrases which indicated to us too heavy a reliance on the standard answer.

Some Words of Caution

We have made an honest attempt to describe the scene on the campuses of the twenty colleges which we visited. Our conclusions are based on literally hundreds of conversations and interviews with students and faculty members. This is what they have told us about themselves and about the great enterprise to which they are devoting their time and energy. We have tried to reflect the flavor which came through the conversations. In some cases, no one quotation could mirror fully the combination of feelings. Where possible, however, we have leaned upon the actual words of students and faculty members.

Naturally some bias is bound to enter, if not in the approach, then in the selection of material to be reported. We have tried to keep this to a minimum. At the same time, however, we conclude with David Riesman that "it will be time enough, after our work is published, for the psychologists to correct us for these oversights, but if we begin by trying to be just to all standpoints we shall lack the courage to be mistaken, the courage to stress something too much."[5]

Included in the text are brief and necessarily limited descriptions of a number of formally organized campus programs. They are, of course, not the only ones we observed, nor are they necessarily unique. Instead, they are programs which came to our attention because of repeated student and faculty allusions to their value.

The Organization of the Report

In the next six chapters we will attempt to describe and illustrate the elements which we identified through our observations as the strongest influences in the development of character in the colleges. No one element stands by itself; all are directly interrelated and interdependent. We will speak of the level of expectancy on a campus and of the concept of teaching as well as the organization of the curriculum. We will discuss how the assumption of responsibility by the student encourages character. We will explore the opportunity for religious understanding and practice. We will then suggest that the campus environment should be a mode of association. In an additional chapter we will open the subject of the selection of appropriate goals by the college.

This is our answer to questions such as these: What is the college's responsibility for and relationship to the character development of its students? How does such a responsibility become related to the professed aim of most colleges to develop and sharpen the intellect? What positive and negative influences on character now operate on the campus? In what direction should the colleges be moving in order to meet the increasing demand for men and women educated for both competence and conscience?

[5] David Riesman, *Constraint and Variety in American Education* (Lincoln, Neb.: University of Nebraska Press, 1956), p. 100.

2. The Level of Expectancy

To my mind college ought to be a really satisfying experience. When we graduate from this old place, we should be proud of our accomplishments, of what we've learned and the way we've performed. Right now, as a senior, I'll have to admit that my four years on this campus have been pretty uneven. Some of the people around here have pushed me so hard that I was amazed I had the stuff in me to respond. Others have engaged in a hit-and-run operation; I'm pretty disgusted with both of us, as I look back on it.

Let me put it this way: where I found weakness, I took advantage of it; but where I found strength, I respected it. If I'm allowed ever to slip by, I'll do it every time. But if I'm really expected to perform. I'll come through or go down fighting.

THE STUDENT was attempting to be honest. His remark occurred in a casual conversation in a dormitory lounge late one evening. We were near the end of our tour of twenty American colleges and universities. But to us his words were not new. Similar testimonies, including some more emphatic and discouraged, had been heard from his counterparts wherever we traveled. It was talk of this kind, listened to early in our study and lasting until the final college had been visited, which led us to identify the implicit as well as the explicit level of expectancy as a highly important determinant of what happens to the college student. Our observations were reinforced by the frequent student reaction echoed by another who concluded, "Oh sure, I've received good marks and all that, but I've never really had to work very hard. Now that it's almost over I feel as though I've been cheating myself, or maybe I've been cheated. I've never really been pushed."

If this level of expectancy is so important, where and how does it begin to operate? We found, as one might expect, that it is cer-

9

tainly not confined to the classroom alone but permeates the living unit, the social life, and all else that comprises the collegiate experience. It begins first in what the college itself hopes to accomplish. The college's stated role should be both honest and possible. If it seeks to do too much, or conversely, too little, it cannot complain if the results are too thinly scattered or too meager.

Out of obligation to its students, the college should assess realistically what it wants to have happen and then expect realistically that the members of its community, students and faculty alike, will work assiduously toward that goal. Those responsible for establishing and carrying out college policy must keep always in mind the range of interests and aptitudes in the student population. Above and beyond a general adherence to excellence, no inflexible level can apply beneficially to all students. Our experiences with students and faculty members suggest that expectations are best established by starting with the student where he is (and that will vary widely) and encouraging him to perform to the outer limits of his capacity (which also will have wide variations).

On the basis of campus conversations, we believe that the college is derelict in its duty if it fails to challenge, to inspire improvement, and, more than this, to *expect* improvement. If the college fails, then it must recognize that subsidiary groups will set the level. On some campuses we visited, the failure was evident to us in the powerful force of such student organizations as fraternities which in effect determine much of what happens to the student and how it shall happen.

The college's expectations are not the result of the thinking of one man alone. No president, for instance, can ever determine by himself what will happen and then expect it to happen. The American college is far too democratic a community to tolerate this for very long. The level is established most successfully in the acceptance by all of a common task, a common goal. It is reached only by the mutual assumption of particular responsibilities. Beyond what the college expects of itself,[1] it must maintain a high but realistic level of expectations of its faculty. The colleges which we visited enunciate common expectations of faculty. One may assume that these are shared by the great majority of all American colleges and universities. We were told, for instance, that the institution should insist that those who teach are those who value, who care intelligently about, the process of education and all that it comprises. The faculty should have the same excitement and enthusiasm for learning which is sought in the student. If the campus is to be the live, provocative community which it aspires to be, the college will recognize and honor the inquiring mind, the quality of intelligent dissatisfaction which leads the scholar not to rest by the academic roadside but continually to push on and on. If the college honestly seeks the truth, it will honor also intellectual integrity as well as vitality. These two are acknowledged to be the chief requisites of a commitment to the quest for truth. As one president commented, "Shakespeare died in 1616; there is no reason why he should be re-buried annually by a spiritless professor."

This is the common agreement. It is, one might propose, easy to pledge allegiance to "the truth." It is far more difficult, however, to carry over attitudes from professional life to personal living. What, for instance, should the college expect in terms of the social and personal behavior of its faculty members? To this question there were many answers. At the least, all agreed on the hope that educated men sense a responsibility and adhere to no less than the social minima (although the minima vary from college to college). Does the college have the right to establish personal standards? We talked with those who felt that it must. In fact, some felt it to be the moral obligation of an institution which pretends to educate leaders. Such standards, however, must be openly arrived at, not arbitrarily imposed. Further, they must be

[1] This is explored in greater detail in chap. 8.

supported both in the original choice of faculty (a difficult and dangerous criterion, many agree) and in the retention and promotion of those who constitute the continuing faculty.

Many faculty members in some institutions (especially those with explicit traditions of freedom) contend that the college has no such right. Furthermore, it can never hope to "police" its staff; therefore, it should not make pretenses in this direction. Nevertheless, these same faculty members profess strong faith in an undefined professional ethic. They, too, want morality in the accepted sense, but they shy away from any semblance of enforcement.

What the college expects of its faculty, then, is in essence what the good faculty member expects of himself. This same generalization applies to what is expected of the student. In the case of the student, however, there is general agreement that a standard can be set high and that it can be enforced. In the establishment of this level the faculty member can and frequently does play an important role. Where examples were cited, both students and faculty referred most often to cheating. It was assumed on every campus that some cheating takes place. In somewhat more than half of the colleges we visited, the assumption was that cheating is more common than most students and faculty members recognize. It extends from copying examination answers to extensive use of dormitory and fraternity files for themes and papers. The student who admits to cheating will admit as readily to specific instances in which he would not consider the act because of the attitude of a particular professor. "That man," we were told by one who mirrored his counterparts, "expects so much of himself and of me that I would never let him down. If I did let him down, I'd go down, too." A second student on the same campus added that he saw no reason not to cheat in another professor's course: "It doesn't make any difference how much work I do; the prof never gives a mark less than a C. With that kind of expectation, I might as well cheat while I concentrate honestly on other subjects."

If the student, buttressed by the institutional and faculty level of expectancy, has a sufficiently high level of self-expectancy, he is ready, under normal conditions, to gain significantly from his collegiate experience. But he cannot expect anything of his education unless he first has hopes for himself. His college experience then becomes the means to realization.

We found that the level of expectancy controls not just academic situations but social relationships, group life, and, in fact, all that happens to the student. It begins, of course, with classroom endeavor, for here is where the college most directly confronts the student.

The Outer Limits

On only a handful of the campuses which we visited did many students claim that they were performing to their full capacity. Those with whom we talked admitted readily that in many ways they were not working hard enough. This conclusion was further strengthened by our direct observation of the amount of time students expend on meaningless activity. Campuses are busy places, but, on analysis, it is surprising to discover how many nonacademically related activities consume the important hours. The ritual of after-dinner bridge is more fact than fiction. A dean of women told us of a survey she had taken of how time was spent by senior women. A sample group kept an hourly account of activities. The dean expressed her amazement at the time consumed by the average in such extended diversions as those associated, for example, with the purchase of toothpaste. "They start downtown at two o'clock to buy the tube and return at five o'clock after two hours or more of coffee and meandering," she observed. "And then they wonder where their study time goes!"

Not a few student leaders have succeeded in establishing their own level. They combine work in the more difficult courses with many hours expended in behalf of campus activities. Their personally set level has taught them the importance of budgeting time.

Students on some campuses ask, not for longer assignments and more detailed outside work, but for study which will challenge and inspire. They voice the seemingly perpetual complaint that their academic work is too trivial and unrelated either to their interests or anything else important. As one student commented, "The solution is not more but better." At the University of Wisconsin, however, a large group of student leaders felt that it was both more *and* better. In the spring of 1958 over two hundred students active in campus affairs fashioned, signed, and sent to the president a petition which, we believe, reflects the sentiments of many students, not just in Madison, but throughout the country. The text of the Wisconsin petition read:

> We undersigned students at the University of Wisconsin are sincerely concerned with the problems faced by the University. It is our belief that students and faculty should work together to find solutions to the problems which are shared alike by all members of the academic community. It is this interest in the community which prompts us to seek your understanding as we strive to make the University of Wisconsin a great academic leader of the nation.
>
> The conclusions we have reached about education at Wisconsin are offered in this light. We believe that no mirror of a university is so adequate as its students, especially its upperclassmen and those who have risen to responsible positions in the student community. We are confident that you need and value insights offered you by students about the University. In a way, we are the yardstick by which you can measure the success of your educational program.
>
> The primary responsibility of any university is to create an academic atmosphere and to engender in its students the desire for knowledge. On the basis of our observations, however, we feel that the University does not hold the position of eminence that it could enjoy in the world of education and that it must step beyond itself into new realms of educational creativity.
>
> Although the University is constantly making attempts to improve its standards, we believe that it has failed to challenge its students sufficiently. In many senses, it is too easy for thousands of students to "get by" and never learn to become critical, analytical thinkers or to achieve an understanding of the world around them. Students on all

levels of attainment feel that they have not worked to the limits of their ability and time.

The University must raise its standards. In some cases this means simply requiring more work; in many more it means emphasizing an improved quality of work and an intelligent, analytical approach to the subject matter.

Students must extend themselves to achieve a deep and meaningful understanding of material. But this is possible only if the faculty seeks to help us by challenging us more fully.

Whenever possible, we think that more courses and examinations should be aimed at challenging students to go beyond mere memorizing and to spend much more time working with and understanding the ideas that are basic to their fields of knowledge.

In more courses definite facilities should be established to enable those students with intensive interest in a subject to probe beyond the attainment requirements of the course, which are in most cases aimed at providing only a general survey of the subject matter.

Facilities should be provided for the students who wish to delve more deeply into the entire subject matter of their particular field, as well as for students who wish to pursue a specific aspect of the course material.

We would like to see more students learn to handle the independent asking and answering of questions which is the only way to a critical understanding of any subject.

We realize that many of us have failed to accept the academic challenge offered by the University. We must accept a good share of the responsibility for our failure to reach the limits of our potential. But the University must assume its measure of responsibility as well. Many standards throughout the University program seriously need a regeneration in excellence.

We hope that secondary schools of the state would be encouraged to follow the lead of the University in raising academic standards.

We are proud of our University for its outstanding record in the graduate field; for its progress in technological fields; and for its defense of intellectual freedom.

We are enthusiastic about the steps which the University is taking to correct some of Wisconsin's serious faults. We believe that these steps will do much to provide a better atmosphere for intellectual growth. Our own student government has made progress with the University in this field.

We ask that this progress be looked at as only a beginning in the creation of a challenging, creative and scholarly atmosphere of academic excellence at the University.

We sign this statement in the belief that a. most important function of education is to encourage serious and constructive criticism.

We trust that our views will be judged in the same serious spirit with which they are given. We hope that at the very least they may provide an index of student opinion which will serve as an impetus to those who determine University policies.

A large majority of the officers, regents, and faculty of Wisconsin wisely and fortunately greeted the petition with interest and a measure of delight. Their reaction stands in contrast to one on another campus who lamented to us, "Students really don't work at learning until they reach graduate school, and then it is largely vocationally inspired. They never give us the chance to liberalize them."

On almost every campus from California to New England, student apathy was a topic of conversation. It was the one subject mentioned most often in our discussions with both faculty members and students. On some campuses it was illustrated by the decline in the number of students who were interested in leadership positions. This was attributed to apathy. When we asked what was meant by apathy, the reply was that "our students seem interested only in getting through with as little effort as possible. Nobody cares any more. Being a leader takes more time than it's worth." A faculty member added his definition: "Apathy is another way of describing the attitude that registers superficial or studied indifference. The unfortunate result is satisfaction with mediocrity."

Some claimed that it is fashionable on a campus to regard work as somewhat disreputable. The student, it appears, should never become excited or involved. We concluded that we should explore further this subject of overriding importance to the college's attempt to develop character. Mediocrity in any form is corrosive to character.

The Encouragement of Excellence

We observed in greater detail those colleges which appeared most to challenge the student and concluded that their efforts were marked by four steps: involvement, application, critical thinking, and commitment.

INVOLVING THE STUDENT

Character development in the American college begins with involvement. Student enthusiasm for learning and for the total collegiate experience starts when the student sees the relationship between himself and what is taught as well as all that happens on a campus. When this takes place, the student loses his attitude of apathy and becomes truly involved in his own learning process. The student, like all human beings, is naturally self-centered. He views education in terms of what it will do *for* him rather than *with* him. We cannot change human nature but we can arrest it from concerns which are strictly narrow and selfish. One faculty member referred to this process as "temptations upward," the continual stretching of the mind and personality to be concerned with more than the selfish and trivial. Involvement does not emerge from trivia.

The inquiring student seeks the broader implications and relationships of what he studies. He frequently complained to us that too few of his teachers begin the encounter by discussing their concept of the over-all purposes of the course, the place it may hold in the student's educational development, its relationship to other subjects, and what it might say to the student as a living, striving person. No matter what the field of endeavor for which the student prepares, that field does have a relationship to fundamental issues. Some students, of course, have greater difficulty seeing that relationship. Bound within themselves, they find security in the isolated and categorizable facts of the particular subject matter. They want nothing more than to be able to assimilate and regurgitate these facts. Locked within many more students, however, is an honest yearning to seek the outer limits of their capacity.

THE HABIT OF APPLICATION

To involvement is added a second characteristic of the college program which conquers apathy. It is acceptance of the habit of careful, honest, and industrious application to academic and personal responsibilities. Our experience with students leads us to conclude that many are not fully cognizant of the demands which true learning should make upon them. They express their bewilderment in frequent complaints that their orientation to the college expectations was inadequate. Further, when they reached college, their introduction to campus expectations took the form of an emphasis on easy adjustment, on as gentle a transition as possible from one level to the next. As one student lamented, "I wanted, but I sure didn't find, a different kind of experience. I had hoped to have drawn from me some new possibilities." Perhaps, it may be concluded, his college succeeded in lowering its expectations to fit the new student rather than engaging in the more difficult task of raising the freshman to the new level.

In our conversations we found many students who professed to seek this substantial break, an experience requiring a sharply ascending level of expectancy. Instead, what proved to be different, in many cases, was the new social freedom and the opportunity to know new friends. A surprisingly large number of students rank social growth as the greatest gain thus far from college. Because the intellectual challenge is not there, they justify continuance of education on this basis. It becomes the center and focus because it is easily recognized and appreciated.

To one who views the college scene, it becomes obvious that the first weeks for the freshman often are not utilized fully for the establishment of expectancy. The student should be introduced to the new level of the campus at the moment he arrives, if not in the literature he reads prior to his application. Several colleges which we observed make a serious and successful attempt to transmit expectations of excellence and integrity during freshman orientation programs, sometimes referred to as Freshman

Week or Welcome Week. Too frequently, however, the emphasis appears to be confined to making "the poor little freshman feel at home" which precludes any work and assumes that fun breeds security. But "home" was never like this, and thoughtful students on a number of campuses recognize and criticize the lack of an introduction to the idea of hard learning. As one observed, "Our energies were drained by a week of singing, shouting, and security-making. And then they expected us to start classes with vim and vigor for learning." If the first impression suggests that the college is a place mainly for making and enjoying friends, some students may never learn the truth that they have enrolled in an institution founded primarily to promote and honor intellectual endeavor.

Some students (and faculty, too) expressed profound dissatisfaction with the obvious neglect of freshman courses. One campus reported with misgivings that over 70 percent of its freshmen are taught by graduate assistants, those ambivalent creatures who push themselves to finish a thesis at the same time they are expected to incite in freshmen a desire for learning.

From our observations we are led to conclude that if the student is to value his learning, he must not receive it easily. A dean with whom we talked stated, "The 'goof off' who gets by through cramming is one who has never learned the basic fact that he is only cheating himself by being satisfied with less than what he could have derived from full-time and thorough immersion in his subject matter." It is important that the student have the experience of exacting and even exhausting work. Most students are quick to discover the minimum necessary "to get by." They discover what is needed both for an A and a C. If the minimum is ridiculously low, the maximum has no appeal. The student who is not challenged soon discovers that he can fritter away much of his study time in the secure conviction that thirty minutes of honest labor will satisfy the professor. His attitude, if allowed to persist, has unfortunate consequences for all that he does, not only his academic work. This is ease, not education, and no education should be easy. Again, like all human beings, the student is quickly and delightedly distracted. We found many students, for instance, on most campuses to be fairly good authorities on current television performers and productions. The student who has not learned to concentrate, to apply himself, borrows too readily from others when the pressure mounts. He has also failed to find and appreciate the ability to do one task at a time and to do it well—completely and thoroughly.

Lest we be misunderstood at this point, we are not advocating what one educator termed "sweat-shop intellectualism." The onerous assignment is no test of learning. The solution obviously is not to expect the impossible. If this becomes the case, the natural student reaction is to discover exactly what the professor considers most important and then concentrate only on that. This will enable one to pass the examination. There is, instead, a balance to be achieved in a realistically high expectation in line with other demands. The student performs at his best when the work is neither too easy nor impossibly difficult.

THE HABIT OF CRITICAL THOUGHT

To involvement and the habit of application we add the concomitant habit of careful, honest, critical thinking. We asked the present-day student how he would describe the ideal person. His answer, for the most part, was first a reflection of society's current concern over the well-adjusted person who can get along with anybody. To this, however, was quickly added education's concern over the person who reasons and acts for himself. The man of character, according to the student, is one who does not accept too readily the point of view of others and yet has the knack of understanding and working with all who cross his path. One junior gave this definition: "I think of a man of character as one who is honest and consistent, who believes in something and doesn't change, and who is well-regarded by everyone." Apparently, then the college faculty which honors and promotes critical thought has made some impact on its students, at least in terms of ideals if not practice. One faculty member linked the quality of critical thought directly to the process of education when he told us, "Unless and until students are forced to reason out and to express the implications of their thoughts, they do not actually learn." As an example, another professor pointed to the ready emotional assumption by students of the completely liberal position on racial problems. But genuine conviction was not present until the students had actually engaged in arguing through the basis of their position or had engaged in some first-hand experiences with racial tensions.

What do faculty members hope for when they establish the expectancy of critical thinking? Initially it is the ability to use logic in the inference of universal principles from particular circumstances and, in like manner, the extraction of the particular from the general. A professor termed it "the identification of a pattern of relationships." Critical thinking helps the student to find values in ideas, to gain humility through understanding, and to respect the rights of others to reach their own conclusions.

We found in the student a strange mixture of the desire for ready answers ("I wish he'd tell us what he wants us to know") and the honest concern for the opportunity to think for himself. The thoughtful student rebels against the course which provides too easily the answer and deprives him of the chance to do his own thinking. But we found too few of these thoughtful students. Perhaps, one might conclude, some faculty members have bowed overreadily to the demand for the easy answer. The instructor in the laboratory, for instance, may have stressed the minutiae of information over the method and attitude of inquiry. He may have failed to recognize the important experience which a course in biology can offer the student in learning that repeated particulars lead to valid generalizations. The instructor's emphasis may have been confined to the particulars, with the scientific method coming out a poor second to the insides of a frog. A dean summarized, "This matter of critical thinking is a responsibility of all of our faculty. Each course, each unit of study, in its own way should make its contribution first to intelligent dissatisfaction and then to logical satisfaction."

THE COMMITMENT TO THE QUEST

Thus far we have identified involvement, application, and critical thinking as characteristics of a high level of expectancy in a college which seeks to engage the student in a new experience of learning. If the student truly identifies himself with what is happening, is willing to expend consuming time and effort, and has begun to master the critical approach, he may then be ready to move on to greater participation in the process of higher learning. The next step of expectancy is the experience of discovering ideas which are larger and more enduring than his once parochial interests. This we term commitment to the quest for greater truth. The task is now big enough to warrant giving one's effort to its fulfillment. This may sound like a noble but slightly jaded sentiment. Nevertheless, our experience moves us to conclude that the college which does not thus encourage its students is both derelict in its duty and hypocritical in its actions in contrast to its stated purpose. The search for truth is, we believe, the answer to the student who asks for a deeper significance to his learning.

Today's student has been criticized for remaining uncommitted, for having no positive concerns of any kind. Perhaps, as one dean commented, "the student is in suspended animation from uncertainty." He is neither uninterested nor immersed. He is expected to believe deeply in at least a few important ideas which are larger than both himself and the subject matter in which he specializes. On this subject a student commented, "Sure, there are a lot of things we don't get excited about, but I don't think it's good to keep getting excited just for excitement's sake.

Then you really haven't got the energy and interest left for the big things that are important." From a different viewpoint, a staff member who had observed students at close range for many years concluded, "Students' convictions are the last lecture they have heard. These convictions in general cover every area. They are just a cross section of adult society's convictions, but they are not very set. The next lecture they hear may change them."

Students readily admit their lack of aroused commitment but they claim they are not helped by a faculty with confined interests. According to some students with whom we talked, many professors ask only for a commitment limited to a particular discipline—the one to which the professor is himself committed, of course. The student rejects this approach as too narrow. It is, to him, a quest only from the viewpoint of the biological sciences, or from the approach of philosophy or psychology, or from the stand of the humanist in literature. One discerning student concluded, "Usually the faculty mean to imply that there are other hitching posts, but you can't blame us for being confused when each one insists on the validity of *his* discipline alone." And his roommate added, "I like to think that truth, whatever it is, is larger than biology or psychology."

If anything marks the students with whom we have conversed, it is their honest search for meaning. And the search is not an easy one because most students are just beginning to sense the dimensions of truth. A student at the University of Colorado wrote in the magazine section of the campus newspaper, "I do not know what I want out of life—or what I want to contribute to life—but I am learning. First I had to learn that it was necessary to have some idea about these questions. It did not take me long to discover that there are no simple answers." If the student as a result of his college experience has failed to realize in some measure the importance of this search and the satisfaction from commitment to it, he has lost a quality which would serve him well in all that he does. An assistant professor of English told us,

"They hide their ideas under a crusty layer of nonconcern, but their English compositions, for instance, show a sensitive searching. Teachers should capitalize on this when discussing themes with them."

Having begun to master the art of thinking critically and having committed himself to the quest, the student soon learns that a certain consistency should mark both his thoughts and his actions. A junior recalled, "Before I came to college I had never considered that good, logical ideas come in orderly progression. I relied on my common sense to tell me which one to jump to next." A professor of philosophy spoke of consistency in this way:

If I hold a position where I say one thing now and five minutes later I say something incompatible with it, if I say things that simply do not jibe with what I say at other times and in other places and contexts, if I contradict myself over and over again, in effect I really don't say anything. I have taken no stand. One statement cancels out the other. If we haven't consistency, we have only a group of opinions flocked together incidentally and accidentally. This is something like doves in a dove-pen. But these doves don't like each other very much and so pretty soon they fly away. In the last analysis, an approach like this is bare of all significance.

SHARED CONVICTION ON THE CAMPUS

Our observations lead us to believe that the student rises best to the challenge in a campus climate marked by a shared conviction which gives broad direction to both the short- and long-range goals of all. We found it refreshing to come upon a campus marked by such conviction. In contrast is the college in which faculty and students may have determined what they individually want but are fairly ignorant of the aims of their colleagues as well as the higher aims of all education. In such an institution a student observed, "This college is composed of a bunch of little circles and each one is revolving in its own little world, not caring what the other ones do; in fact, ridiculing what they do. There is no over-all unity."

The shared commitment to the quest implies an assumption of

responsibility by all for all. Each is obligated to make his special contribution in his own particular way, but all are expected to contribute. For both students and faculty this becomes a campus of which it is a pleasure, not a drudgery, to be a part. Something akin to excitement and challenge is happening. We talked with one freshman early in his first year. He confided, "It's a funny thing around here. You're supposed to be blasé and sophisticated and never get enthused. But I can't help it. I like this place—and do you know why? Because both the students and the faculty admit they don't have all the answers but they'll do their damnedest to get them. I feel as though I ought to help, too."

Properly nourished, shared conviction makes a rewarding adventure of education and deepens the interest of the student beyond the mere superficiality of the experience for the degree's sake. It implies a genuine preference for quality and truth. It places a premium on excellence as a part of what is expected. The satisfaction one gains from knowing he is doing his best is an experience too frequently missing on many campuses. Here is one contribution of substantial proportion which the college experience can make available to the student.

We have found what we believe to be a direct relationship between the depth of the desire for excellence and the general morale of a campus. Several colleges which we visited were marked by a pervading dissatisfaction with anything less than the best. To be at work in such a climate is itself a productive experience, genuinely gratifying to both students and faculty. Such a college is devoid of the second-rate complex which often results in second-rate endeavor. A faculty member at one college complained, for instance, "This school just doesn't think big enough. One day it tries to maintain the status quo, and the next it tries to imitate the old-line Eastern colleges." We visited many types and many sizes. Naturally, all could not be intent upon the same goals through the same methods, But, regardless of the type or size, it is possible, we believe, for a college to be distinctive within its own chosen limits. And if the college believes it can be distinctive and works toward that distinction, those who are a part of it soon adopt the same attitude.

Shared conviction of the right sort enables the student to keep a sense of proportion among his concerns. He can identify himself with something larger than the purely personal. A professor of history summarized, "The important thing for a student to learn in college is a sense of excitement and feeling for life. If one really captures this feeling, it automatically leads to a sense of social responsibility. It draws a person out of himself into a realization of other people." We have observed that where student dissatisfaction leads to overabundant criticism and sometimes to demonstrations and riots over minor matters of regulations and rules, the campus obviously has encouraged too limited an outlook as well as competition among fragmental interests. The students have failed to sense the essential purpose of the enterprise.

The commitment to the quest is, of course, a continuing one. The search never ends. The associated character values, too, are never attained at any given point. The good student is not that easily satisfied. The 1957 yearbook of the University of Wisconsin captioned a picture with this comment: "If the University has taught the individual not to expect an end in four years, he will go out more prepared to study than he was the night he crammed for his last exam." Education becomes an intelligent adventure with new rewards and challenges at each turn of the road.

These, then, are the characteristics which we have identified as important to the maintenance of a high level of expectancy: involvement, application, critical thinking, and commitment to the quest for greater truth. They are, we believe, the effective answer to corrosive apathy. The student who is bored in his classroom work either transfers this wearisome attitude to other phases of campus life or finds fresh new outlets for his energies and interests. We have found strong indication that when he lacks genuine concern for all that surrounds him and is devoid of any real enthusiasm over what is happening to him, he is then subject to the passing whim. Boredom in academic life may tend also to smother creativity in all of life. We have already mentioned the frequent instances of the student leader who found time for outside responsibilities in the midst of carrying a difficult and challenging academic load. As one student told us, "When I like a course, I really plunge in and get the work done. And then I look around for more to do. After this, I discover that keeping busy is a pretty good way to live. I guess that's why I enjoy my part in student government. Some of my friends tell me that I'm gung-ho about everything, but I'd rather be that way than miss all the things in college life that they do."

A primary task of the college in character development is to give the student the incentive to move out from his once narrow confines into challenges which require the best of his many talents. These challenges help to reveal in him both his strengths and weaknesses, an important lesson which the colleges could teach more often to both over- and under-confident young people. The student learns also to live for something beyond the here and now. As one faculty member told a group in which we participated, "If we are preoccupied with ourselves and our immediate problems, and if we try to solve these problems in terms of the unfortunate demands of the immediate present alone, then we shall solve nothing. We shall fail to meet our responsibilities to ourselves or to anyone or anything else."

Establishing and Maintaining the Level

Establishing and maintaining a higher level of expectancy is no easy task. Though the expectancies may be explicitly stated, the pursuit comes only when the level is reflected in the entire campus atmosphere. For this reason, we are led to conclude that academic levels of expectancy are insufficient if they stand alone, devoid of support from a similarly high level of dormitory and fraternity life, campus activities, and social relationships.[2] This, however, is an especially difficult problem for the nonresidential college. For a level to be operative, or, for that matter, for any character influences to take effect, the faculty of the nonresidential college must assume a proportionately larger share of the responsibility. We have visited a large urban university and an urban junior college. From our experiences we would estimate that the faculty in these institutions have a particularly demanding role to play in the lives of the students, and one which is substantially greater than in the residential college.

Different levels of expectancy are apparent at different types of institutions. In chapter 8 we will discuss the appropriate goals of the institution. It is sufficient to say here, however, that we believe there is abundant evidence to indicate that the college can establish its own level and it can, with some concentrated effort, raise that level. In several colleges we noted, for instance, in response to our conversations with lowerclassmen as compared with upperclassmen, a more than usual difference in attitude and apparent achievement. On further examination we found a conscious effort on the part of the college to lift the quality of its endeavor. We proceeded to examine in greater detail how this was accomplished. Certain components of action became apparent.

Obviously, as we have stated, the climate of the campus is the key to expectations. It is an amorphous totality of implicit and explicit factors. In addition to academic standards, it includes concepts and methods of teaching, conduct of campus affairs, social activities, and organizational life. The college which seeks to raise the level begins, we believe, by eliciting the support of all those who are in part responsible for the common life. This includes the governing body of trustees or regents, the administrative officers, the members of the faculty, and appropriate stu-

[2] Environment is discussed in full in chap. 7.

dent groups as well as individual students. Unless a majority of the persons in each of these categories assents to the new emphasis, there will result unfortunate divisive elements which prevent the new level from becoming accepted fully. Each must be willing to face the consequences in terms of particular responsibilities. The trustees, for instance, may expect greater pressure from those who are unhappy with the effect. The administrative officers, including personnel deans and advisers, will be forced to make some apparently arbitrary decisions, particularly in contrast to previous decisions. The faculty members will need to look to themselves and to guard carefully lest they take the easier path of requiring merely longer assignments. And those students who come principally to take away a diploma may grumble and groan. The lifting of the level must be, however, a common effort, not the isolated working of one man or a single group of men.

The next step involves both the initial choice of new members of the faculty and staff as well as the criteria for recognition and promotion of the continuing members. This, too, must be a goal shared by all. We observed one example, for instance, of a president who established in his own mind new criteria without first gaining the assent and understanding of those under him who draw up the list of new candidates and make the first decisions regarding the promotion of the continuing faculty. Needless to say, through misinterpretations, all kinds of motives were attributed to the attitude and actions of the president.

A parallel step follows in the choice of students. If they so choose, most colleges are free to raise admissions requirements or provide new emphases. But this must be done with care. Admissions requirements always run the danger of any artificial screening device. We spent some time at one particular college which has an established reputation for the idealism of its students. Research methods have been used to uncover how and why students *gain* this quality. The president gave us one answer when he stated frankly and openly that "this is the kind of student we select. I don't think we really do much more than make sure the college doesn't rob him of the quality during his four years with us." His confession must be accepted for its humility. Our observations would lead us to believe, however, that even this task of the college is a most difficult one. Nevertheless, the institution did operate from an initial advantage because of its admissions criteria.

Another essential activity in raising a level is one often neglected in many colleges—a continuing self-examination and appraisal. It extends from constant review of the curricular offerings to stimulating students to undertake a similar, continuing review of living units and activities. Perhaps because students are campus transients, they are less prone to uproot traditional groups and events. On most campuses which we visited students cited numerous activity groups which served little or no function, or whose functions might profitably be combined with other groups. But few professed a willingness, in accepting leadership of a particular group, to be the one to allow it to die.

Finally, the level must be enforced. If it is commonly agreed upon as a goal, then there should be little hesitation about taking the steps which will make it an actuality. Several students at one college agreed that "Here they mean business. As Prexy often tells us, 'The door opens out as well as it opens in.'" Some natural attrition in the student body as well as among faculty members will help. But it is folly to say *we* are going to work toward *this* and then allow expediency and extenuating circumstances to divert the effort. One more word needs to be said regarding attitude. The level cannot be achieved if it smacks of paternalism. On all campuses, students are told they are adults. They respond, we believe, when action follows description.

FACULTY-STUDENT UNDERSTANDING

In both their formal and informal contact with students, faculty members reflect the implicit expectations. The very example which the faculty member sets as a person is important to student recognition of what is expected of him. The faculty member who is careless and apathetic can expect the same response from his students. One student, for instance, mentioned that a particular member of the faculty always hounded his class to do its work thoroughly and on time. But, according to the student, "the professor himself didn't bother to cover the material of the course during the year. Instead he tried to do it in the final examination!"

To be effective, faculty members should take into account their own motivations as well as the student motivations which deeply condition student response. As one faculty member noted, "I wonder sometimes if many of my students aren't asking for something from their learning which I'm not prepared to give— something which occasionally is almost foreign to my concept of the real business of education." Naturally, the faculty member cannot expect the young and inexperienced to grasp and accept immediately what the experienced wants. On the other hand, there may be a wider gap than many faculty members wish to acknowledge.

The results of a study completed last year by the University of New Hampshire Counseling Service indicate that often students and faculty members do not really understand each other; their goals are strikingly divergent. The study concludes that students and faculty want different things from a college education. On a rating scale students placed vocational preparation, social growth, and the degree for the degree's sake significantly higher than did the faculty. Faculty members, on the other hand, ranked intellectual growth and informal intellectual activity significantly higher than did the students. A third cluster of values, including self-fulfillment, self-understanding, and preparation for life, formed a meeting ground. The authors of the study observe:

Concern with the intellect and associated activities tower high in the need structures and self-images of most university professors. It is only natural that they would tend to perceive and to structure their worlds in these terms. Similarly, the culture which produced the students, and to which most of them will return, is overwhelmingly characterized by concerns of social, economic, and vocational expediency.[3]

The New Hampshire study indicated further that, as students progress through college, they fail to show any increasing awareness of, or agreement with, faculty goals. Seniors, for instance, were as inadequate as freshmen in the ability to predict what the goals of faculty might be. The study concluded that "communication between the groups may be limited, and of such quality as to induce little or no increase in mutual acceptance."

We have been particularly fascinated by not infrequent examples of *student* expectations which are sufficiently high to raise the level of the faculty. The petition from student leaders at the University of Wisconsin reflects, we believe, an interesting trend. On several other campuses we found similar movements to raise the level, although none had become as explicit as Wisconsin. The subject of how long and when the library should be open was under heated debate, for example. Students fought the library staff and those responsible for its budget in an effort to make the facilities more available. One student lamented to us, "They keep that building closed all day Sunday—the one day when we're not tied up in classes." Students in at least three other of the twenty colleges and universities voiced sometimes intense dissatisfaction with the inadequacy of their learning experience, with the inflexibility of the curriculum, and with the insensitive attitude of some of the professors. One disgruntled student wrote the following letter to the editor of his student newspaper:

The Wednesday before Thanksgiving I had six hours of scheduled classes. One instructor held class as usual, another dismissed the class about half way through and the rest didn't even show up. "Free cut," they say, and give you a big smile.

[3] By permission of the authors, Frederick M. Jervis and Robert G. Congdon, from "Student and Faculty Perceptions of Educational Values," *American Psychologist*, XIII (1958).

. . . I'm paying over a dollar an hour in tuition for each class—and that doesn't include the other expenses of school such as fees, room and board. This is a free cut? I've had five of these expensive free cuts in one class alone.

Everyone knows the vital importance of social activities in building an all-around Joe College, but it seems this hyper-vacation policy is making an ass out of the sporting life. Hark to the call of . . . Thanksgiving—and it's time for a few more cuts. . . .

I need my class time. I can't read Plato and interpret him, and the textbook explanation of anticyclonic vorticity is hopeless. . . . The instructors here are very good, but nevertheless they are hired for the benefit of the students—aren't they? The University owes me about $25. I'll settle for a little education.

Most students with whom we talked were not fully aware of the influence which is at their command. They have the opportunity to help broaden the horizon of the more narrow faculty member, to force him to delve more deeply and to cherish more fully. One student reported, "In one of my classes the students agreed we weren't working hard enough. The treatment was superficial. We ganged up on the prof and shot so many questions at him that he had to go back and take a second look at his own knowledge as well as his method."

THE ROLE OF TRADITION

In some colleges and universities, tradition maintains the level of expectancy. The level attracts because of itself. Radcliffe College, for example, maintains a high level of academic expectancy. For the most part, students perform according to this standard because they choose the college anticipating what is expected. Students and faculty repeatedly indicate that it is the tradition. "This," they say, "is Radcliffe, take it or leave it." Oberlin College and Wesleyan University are other examples of institutions recognizing the constructive influence of tradition.

The level of expectancy is established by the college's past and maintained by the students who select the particular institution on the basis of present expectation based on past performance.

Relatively few colleges enjoy the quality of traditional intellectual excellence. Every institution, however, has the potential to develop its own special tradition. Once it becomes known and maintained, it is not easily disregarded. It is a potent force in attracting students and faculty who are willing to perform according to the tradition.

The positive approach in expectancy is often supplemented by the use of, or threat of the use of, disciplinary action. Properly employed, a pressure such as this can be a constructive influence. The program of the United States Naval Academy is an example of articulate and outspoken expectancy of students, involving pride and fear to help accomplish its goal. Each midshipman, for instance, is conditioned to feel great pride in wearing the uniform of and in being a Navy man. As one stated, "We *must* act like gentlemen. The public expects us to and they observe every move we make." Such an approach does, of course, work more successfully in a military atmosphere or in a college with strong disciplinary orientation. It cannot be introduced quickly and forcefully into a campus long accustomed to greater freedom and less accountability.

PLANNED CAMPUS PROGRAMS

The level of expectancy is made known in a variety of ways. Among these are planned programs emphasizing institutional expectations as a whole. Any program dealing with character runs into immediate difficulty in the definition of terms. We observed, however, that concern over the subject and continuing attempts to deal with it often in themselves account for whatever success and influence the program may enjoy. On the following pages we will describe several which were operative on campuses which we visited.

An example of an explicit, structured program is the emphasis at Stephens College on the Ten Ideals. Through group effort, the students of Stephens, with faculty guidance, attempt to define the kind of person each student should strive to become. It is important to note that the Ten Ideals program is indigenous to the particular type and size of college which Stephens is and to the climate of that two-year institution with its stronger than usual attention to the whole person. The program is not something which can be inserted superficially into the emphasis of another institution; it has been developed over the years at Stephens. The quick, sure thing is never very permanent. At Stephens the Ten Ideals appear to constitute more than the usual statement which is penned, printed, and forgotten.

In the selection of the Ten Ideals, the Stephens students have formulated what some call a "design for living." The following qualities were chosen as basic goals in behavior: appreciation of the beautiful, cheerfulness, courtesy, forcefulness, health, honesty, love of scholarship, self-discipline, service, and reverence toward the spiritual.

Over the years the students attempt to develop ways to make the Ten Ideals more personal and attainable in their lives individually and as they live and work together. Among the methods adopted has been the practice of featuring in the yearbook pictures of girls chosen as representative of each of the ideals (in lieu of the usual beauty queen roster). Also, a Ten Ideals Emphasis Committee has been formed within the student government to carry on activities designed to promote understanding and practice of the ideals. Through the efforts of this committee, each of the ideals is evaluated and more concrete methods developed to encourage the practice of each one.

Annually the students form a secret committee to choose the ten representatives. A number of girls described this activity as a particularly significant experience. Each member strives for objective understanding of others' behavior in living up to these qualities. Students also pointed to many evidences of the interest in the ideals and of activities stemming from them. For example, the Emphasis Committee recommendations made one year ago on such matters as bulletin board displays and clarification and publication of the ideals were adopted almost *in toto*. As one faculty member stated proudly, "Administrative support and student concern don't rest with theory; they extend to actual attempts to promote living what is professed."

In our conversations and interviews, many Stephens students referred to the ideals as important in their developing appreciation of themselves and of others. Strong interest was shown throughout the campus. The program is in keeping with the particular emphases of the college.

We found the community atmosphere at Saint Mary's College in Notre Dame, Indiana, to be another example of an indigenous emphasis. It is related directly to the comparatively small size of the college and the religious homogeneity which places the student in the position of becoming fairly easily a participating member of the community. She is expected to work toward common goals and to abide by common restrictions, much as members of a family do.

At Goddard College in Vermont the small size of the student body (numbering less than one hundred) contributes to the effectiveness of the community government program. Faculty and students work toward establishing and maintaining community standards. The "community" consists of all students, faculty members, administrative and maintenance staff members, and their spouses. The government is a distinct administrative unit within the college framework, handling large areas of responsibility delegated to it by the college administration and trustees. Included are the creation and enforcement of rules and standards for community living, the administration and supervision of the campus work program, and the college's recreational activities, as well as a continuing review of educational practices in the college. This extends to evaluation of the work of each faculty member.

Officers in the Goddard government are chosen from the campus at large. It is not uncommon for faculty members to run against students for the same office. Faculty members serve on each committee except the all-student group concerned with educational policies. The heart of the community government is the community meeting held twice each month. Formally, the meeting is the legislative assembly of the government; informally, it is a forum for the discussion of many aspects of Goddard life.

Many signs and symbols on campuses are explicit illustrations of implicit expectations. It is impossible, of course, to measure how profound the influence may be, but Americans everywhere do live by slogans; the colleges should not be denied their right to do so. The library at one state university warns, "Who Knows Only His Own Generation Remains Always a Child," while the same structure at another institution bears the biblical promise, "You Shall Know the Truth, and the Truth Shall Make You Free." Many of the faculty members and students with whom we talked at the University of Wisconsin mentioned the strong and pervasive dedication of that institution to the principles of academic freedom. A surprising number voluntarily introduced into the conversation the concepts couched in the Wisconsin Board of Regents' statement of 1894: "Whatever may be the limitations which trammel inquiry elsewhere, we believe that the great State University of Wisconsin should ever encourage that continual and fearless sifting and winnowing by which alone the truth can be found."

At another institution the word freedom was linked with responsibility in a concept frequently mentioned by students and administrative officers. But overuse and resulting weakness of the symbolism became apparent when one of the major administrative officers told us that he hoped never again to hear the phrase. He had become disgustedly tired of it.

On some campuses the continuing struggle for academic freedom has served to sharpen in students' minds the basic issues regarding the purposes of educational institutions. The question of whether or not to bring controversial speakers to a campus has stimulated consideration of the principles involved. The University of New Hampshire, for example, received the first Alexander Meiklejohn Award for "responsible educational statesmanship" as demonstrated by permission given to a student group to sponsor a particularly controversial speaker. The award came from a national organization, the American Association of University Professors. The honor immediately was condemned by the governor of New Hampshire and the conservative attorney general of the state. Student reaction indicated genuine dismay over the lack of confidence on the part of public officials in the right of students to hear discussion of controversial questions and in their ability to discriminate among choices. The willingness of the president and a majority of the board of trustees to accept the award in the face of such strong criticism made more vivid to the students why their university existed and what was expected from members of an academic community.

WHERE HIGHER VALUES FLOURISH

On the basis of our visits to twenty colleges and universities, we are deeply impressed with the overriding importance of the level of expectancy on a campus. It exercises a control over all phases of the college experience, not just the strictly academic work. The level applies to all that happens to the student. If nothing more than mediocrity is rewarded, students will not lift their sights. The college sometimes tends to take for granted the student who believes in working toward increasingly higher standards and principles. It busies itself with threatening or punishing those who fall below the mean rather than finding ways to recognize and encourage those who do achieve. A more positive emphasis might well reduce the number of those who wander aimlessly and fail from lack of inspiration.

The success of any character development emphasis rests first, then, on the level of expectancy. The college *can* expect more of its students. As one educator notes, "Often we ask too little and expect less." The expectation begins with the college itself, extends to the faculty, and culminates in the student. It rests on the conviction held in common by faculty and students that higher learning demands and deserves the highest possible excellence. In such an atmosphere, the members of the academic community will strive together to maintain a campus on which the higher values flourish. We believe that this is at once the first and most significant contribution of the college to the character of its students.

3. *The Concept of Teaching*

It seems unfortunate that the most important part of what ought to be reported cannot be, for lack of any tool of evaluation. Having been even busier than usual at classroom activities, we would ask: To what end? We believe we have raised some important questions with enough impact so that some of our students have started seeking answers. We believe we have encouraged some of them to reject simple answers to complex problems and to recognize the labor and discomfort that are often the price that must be paid for understanding.

With perhaps a considerable number of students who have attended our classes, the results may well have been less fruitful than they expected. Our majors have, however, matured in a way one would wish and we like to think their association with us and with each other in our classes helped. To remove our bias, we can only say: Here are our seniors; think back to when they were freshmen and sophomores. If there is a change for the better, we probably had something to do with it; it represents in large part the results of our activities in teaching that particular college generation.

IN THIS WAY and with these mixed emotions, a department chairman in one of the institutions made his report to the dean. His thoughtful, bittersweet statement reflects the searching we found in good teachers everywhere to discover that spark which, in its mysterious way, lends a quality of excellence to a student's education.

In this chapter we explore the concept of teaching. The great majority of students in all the colleges and universities which we visited spoke frequently and freely of the impact of the good teacher on their lives. We mention "good" because it is obvious from the record of their conversations that mere teaching by itself guarantees no solid reaction. Only under certain conditions and only when certain qualities are present in the man and his method do students respond positively. We shall attempt to spell out those conditions and qualities.

Early in the study, as a result of our initial visits and interviews, it became evident to us that the college cannot hope to fulfill its obligation to character development without unusual attention paid both to the teacher and to his idea of teaching. The teacher was cited frequently and voluntarily as an integral part not just of learning in its narrow sense but of the broader kind of education which leads to character modification. We asked, then, what are these qualities of the teacher? What does the student say about the teachers he regards most highly? Our method was simple. On each campus which we visited, certain members of the faculty were identified repeatedly in our conversations with students and with other faculty members and administrators. We made it a point, then, to seek out these people, to talk with them about what they do and how they do it, about their own incentives and concerns.

We found at once that those who were singled out were not necessarily the more experienced, not always the elder statesmen of the campus. Nor, surprisingly enough, was a personal confrontation essential to the student's respect and admiration. As one student pointed out, "I get to know the prof first through the classroom. If I like him enough, I make sure then that I seek him out, either during his office hours or in some outside contact. Maybe he leads a discussion someplace and then I go. Or maybe I make sure my dorm invites him to visit us."

The faculty members who were identified and with whom we talked almost unanimously accepted some degree of responsibility for the character education of their students. And they were equally affirmative in believing that it cannot be a consciously planned effect. As one commented, "Once you are too self-conscious of what you are doing, all opportunity for real value teaching has been destroyed." A dean repeated his warning: "As a teacher, don't try to do too much for your students. Set the spark and the student will catch fire where he is inflammable." The chief purpose of college education is, according to the majority, the training of the intellect. The end product should be a wise and thoughtful person who knows that his education is really just beginning and that it is a lifelong process. In the strongly church-centered institutions, many faculty members couple the training of the intellect directly with an explicit value structure. In the secular institutions they phrase it as the education of concerned and responsible citizens. But the point is that something besides pure intellectual training is accepted as an obligation. Not all agree openly, of course. One told us, "This amorphous character stuff is the job of the personnel people. I'll let them worry about it. I teach history, and that's my job." On further exploration, however, we discovered that this man was one of the most influential and highly regarded in the entire faculty. As a personnel dean told us, "Sure, he may think it's our job. But we build on his solid foundation. We'd be helpless without the kind of contact he makes with students. If we pointed this out to him, however, he'd be shocked."

Commitment and Objectivity

We found unanimous agreement among students on the particular approach which the good teacher makes. Whatever the type of institution, its students appear to value far more highly the faculty member who is willing to make known his own commitments. He should not expect the student to accept them unexamined, for only by working ideas out himself does the student truly appreciate his newly established position. One faculty member observed, "I prefer not to think of teaching as the inculcation of principles, but as the encouragement to establish one's own set of beliefs." Students agree that often they first recognize the importance of taking a stand after they have actually observed a person who is honestly and carefully committed. Further, they like to know what a faculty member believes and how he approached that belief. Certainly they do not expect the professor to take time from each class to be autobiographical, nor do they want him to state anything but the plain, unvarnished truth about himself. It is only when the position has relevance to the subject matter or approach to the subject matter that students want it introduced into the class. On the other hand, they sense immediately and are suspicious of any faculty member who tries to hide under a blanket of assumed objectivity.

Some faculty members expressed genuine surprise at this student expectation. They voiced the strong feeling that most students with whom they have had contact do not come to college to learn about and assess various positions. To the contrary, they are interested only in substantiating their prejudices. In this regard, as a side comment, it is interesting to note that some of the faculty members who hold to this belief apparently see no connection between their own attitudes and what they describe as inadequate student incentives.

Many of the students with whom we talked appeared to be confused by the attempt of some faculty members always to remain completely objective. They wondered, for instance, why faculty members complain so bitterly about the student's noncommitment at the same time that the faculty encourage the student to suspend his judgment. One student leader concluded, "We're called the 'silent generation,' but can you really blame us? We've studied under those who often make a fetish of silence." It is apparent, therefore, that faculty should make plain to the student that one can be committed to certain values and still be objective in his teaching. As one professor noted, "Being too objective is sometimes like having a hole in your head," while another stated, "One can't be purely objective all the time unless he is a fool or a liar." A report of the Harvard Student Council commented:

Students frequently receive the impression that this noncommitted, objective stance is the only one that is scholarly and scientific. Hence they may think that they should try to maintain it all of the time, even when commitment is in order. . . . If suspended judgment is connected with a scholarly approach, students may remain suspended until they leave the academic community, and then revert to earlier social norms or unthinkingly adopt new ones offered them by the society they enter.

What appears important, therefore, is that the student not receive the impression that faculty members have no fixed beliefs, but that their beliefs came about through logical processes of thought, devoid of snap judgments and easy rationalization to accommodate long-standing prejudices.

In some colleges student groups have attempted to offer platforms to the faculty member to encourage him to make known his commitments. On almost every campus, for instance, we found that students were interested in informal discussions with faculty in the living units. During these discussions the students felt a freedom in their own familiar setting to ask the faculty member more searching questions about his concepts and concerns.

On a number of campuses, Mortar Board, the senior women's honorary society, has sponsored a series of lectures directed to this end. It is sometimes called the "Last Lecture." Faculty members who agree to participate are asked to prepare a talk which is, in essence, a summing-up—a presentation of what they might say to their students if they knew this were to be their last opportunity to address a student group. Each faculty member presents his views in the form he chooses. Some explore a universal idea of significance to them and then urge its continuing consideration. Others discuss vignettes of their lives including influences which have changed and enriched them. The Last Lecture, though not always successful or popular, is an illustration of student interest in faculty commitment.

We have noted also the positive influence of the unorthodox thinker on a campus. We believe that it is desirable from the student point of view to have a mixture of views and ideas. As one student told us, "That man has the craziest notions about people and life, but by having them he's stimulated more students to think. Although we almost always come out rejecting what he says, as a result we do believe far more firmly in our own point of view." Under many professors of varying persuasions, the student will encounter a variety of convictions instead of repeated instances of watered-down objectivity.

Devotion to the Subject

The good teacher acts as a catalyst. He introduces the student to the subject matter in such a way that the student is moved to explore on his own. From student comments we would gather that the teachers held in highest regard are those who possess that rare combination of wisdom and sensitivity which attracts learners around them and captures the enthusiasm which is so characteristic of the young. Without this wisdom and this caring in the teacher, the student feels no incentive to acquire more than the minimum necessary to pass the course. The student has no lasting interest in studying under the teacher who pampers and coddles. Those teachers who were identified and with whom we talked were often the most demanding.

Such teachers, furthermore, were marked by a strong passion for the subject matter in which they specialized. As one noted, "The only way in which a teacher can reach his responsibility to his students or to himself is by aiming at something else, and that something else is his subject." He himself must be interested, excited, and eager to continue expanding his admittedly incomplete knowledge. The love of subject is accompanied by a deep humility in its presence and a deep honesty in its presentation. Misrepresentation has no place in the classroom, and faculty admit that most students are quick to uncover and reject the teacher who is anything less than honest. "The word" about certain professors soon becomes known on a campus.

The secret of the teacher's task appears to lie in his desire and then his ability to pass on some of that passionate interest to others. There is always, of course, the constant danger of the teacher becoming so involved that he forgets this obligation. A not infrequent observation of students was, "I guess he knows his subject. But I often wonder if it's really clear in his own mind when he can't seem to make it clear to any of us." There is danger, too, in a dependence on personality alone. It is almost a magic formula which combines the respect of the student with the warmth which allows the student to identify himself with the teacher. About one frequently mentioned faculty member a student noted, "He always treats people as human beings, never misuses them. He's both intelligent and thoughtful—and that means a lot to the students. We feel as though he knows we're all different and he tries to stimulate the difference by bringing out our individual potentialities." Concluding his observations on teaching, a widely recognized scholar told us, "The assumption of the teacher is that interest in truth is presently locked in every human being; and that it will respond to any genuine presentation of the real article."

The word "genuine" assumes great importance to the student. Learning is a partnership, a fascinating adventure for both student and teacher. The manner in which the teacher works is observed carefully by the discerning student. A student columnist in the campus newspaper wrote this tribute to one of her professors: "Dynamic behind a lectern, he injects students with both fear and inspiration when they visit his office. But for all his knowledge he is not pretentious. He accepts students who have achieved something as cohorts on the road to a greater understanding of the world we live in." An overzealous attempt to keep the student from making mistakes often backfires. One professor told us that he never taught a class without telling the students about the one time when he considered he had been really dishonest. And one of his students later mentioned that this was "a pretty embarrassing class session. Everybody knows it's coming and we all steel ourselves for it. But I guess the old boy does have to get it out of his system."

The successful teacher becomes in a sense a living reflection of what he teaches—something above and beyond the mere facts. In the words of one, "If the teacher doesn't believe it, and doesn't show that he believes it, and if he doesn't live as if he believes it, then certainly nobody else will." Through his zest and enthusiasm the teacher brings life and vitality to his discipline. A professor of English literature was cited by students as contagiously enthusiastic about her subject. When we talked with her, she said, "I try to stimulate the class by digging into things, trying to find out why the author felt this way, trying to catch the emotion. You know, really throwing inhibitions aside and shouting when the story shouts, and laughing when it laughs. It's unfortunate when students get a feeling of propriety which isn't manners. It is, instead, just a deadening of feelings and emotions."

Since searching for truth is an endless quest, the good teacher appears never to be ashamed to search before his students. If his search is honest, he has no reason to hide. He should want unquestionably to share with his students the beauty which he has found thus far. He should want them to partake of its significance. His faith in his subject, his faith in his students, and his concern for integrity will soon inspire the student. Then come, in the words of Nathan Pusey, those "moments of heightened insight [and] rare experiences of great excitement" which suddenly make education take on increased relevancy to life.

Setting an Example for Students

When we asked the student to give an illustration of an incident or relationship which had profoundly affected his attitude toward life, frequently he cited a particular faculty member. One student, for instance, commented, "Professor X in his teaching and just in his very being has given my life more purpose and direction than any other person I know. My three years so far on this campus have been worth that one contact." The student appears quick to sense the positive potentialities in human beings which are reflected in his teachers. For the most part we found students everywhere to be both impressionable and flexible. They appeared ready and indeed anxious to be influenced. And even the most casual kind of encounter can have an effect. On the negative side, for example, several students on different campuses mentioned that they had changed their majors and thus potentially the course of their lives because a department head had left an impression that it made no difference whatsoever to him whether or not a student wanted to specialize in the particular subject matter to which he had devoted his life. Other students, however, were equally emphatic in stating that they had chosen a subject field principally because of the men who taught it.

A number of faculty were reticent about discussing directly the personal effect of the teacher, lest in the very discussion the magic be destroyed. On the other hand, some looked upon it as maudlin sentimentality. It is interesting to note, however, that our conversations with faculty revealed the overriding importance which they themselves place upon the influence of their teachers. We asked faculty members also to illustrate an incident or relationship profoundly affecting their lives. The answer frequently included a teacher who through personal interest, or as an example of integrity or of devout scholarship, had made a change. Some faculty members, therefore, cited this for themselves but, at the same time, shied away from their responsibility to the next generation. There is a protective device in maintaining one's neutrality and distance. An assistant professor stated, "I hate this idea that I'm on display all the time. When I want to get drunk, I don't want to think there are five hundred kids acting as my conscience." Another faculty member observed, "You know, I sometimes wonder what effect there will be on the student from the continuing faculty talk of inadequate salaries. We may leave them with the impression that all we care about is material gain!"

Faculty members in many colleges and universities which we visited cited the demands upon their time as reason for their inability to work more closely with students. One stated derisively, "If we're going to serve as moral tutors, the administration had better allow us some extra time or there won't be much morality." His comment in the extreme did reflect, however, a concern among many over the increasing emphasis in colleges on time devoted to research and publication as a measure of achievement. Most of those with whom we talked acknowledged the obligation of faculty to undertake research and to publish as a means of keeping current in their subject field and of adding to man's store of knowledge. But they were unhappy over the system of priorities in their own colleges as well as the basis for employment in other colleges which they hoped might be interested in them.

This is especially onerous, some claimed, because the time of a faculty member is also spread among other responsibilities. And examples were cited of committee work, community activities, participation in special college projects, extraclass life, learned societies, and outside consultation work. An associate professor complained, "When you get right down to it, we are neither chosen for, nor expected to play, a substantial role in the development of students." He claimed further that all the ancillary tasks are bound to result in professional apathy toward those things which are truly important to the student. At a large university, students voiced pride in a faculty under which, nonetheless, few of them had ever studied. A junior observed, "We're the ones who are cheated because they're always cloistered in their publication and research work. We study under them second-hand. We get their graduate students."

Apparently most faculty members look to the administration of the college to establish the priorities. And the priority starts in the original selection of faculty. If the college honors teaching and the teacher's relationship to the student, in considering a candidate it might well ask what impression as a person this teacher makes. What image of man will he present to the student? A professor of philosophy commented, "We're so careful about the intellectual effect but we fail to provide for the personal. We strive to have different points of view represented but with little regard for the manner of men." A president told us that it was the definite intent of his university to select teachers with high standards and to expect those standards to remain high. All else, except knowledge of subject matter, was secondary. On further questioning, however, he was at a loss to say how this was accomplished. Finally he admitted that it was probably just wishful thinking.

The question of the image of man as represented by faculty members enters also into subsequent recognition and promotion. The college which allows sentiment to become the principal criterion for tenure, for instance, does a disservice not only to its own reputation but to the student who must study under the inadequate professor. We conclude, therefore, that far more than pure knowledge is important in the college's choice of faculty, particularly if the college makes pretenses about character development.

Two other criteria have been identified for us as part of the picture. The degree of intellectual discipline which has bearing upon the conclusions which a faculty member reaches in his subject-matter field is of great importance. In addition one must take note of his attitude. Does he, for instance, exhibit humility in his scholarship? Does his life outlook give meaning, perspective, and rationale to his career? Does he really like people? These are admittedly difficult questions to answer but substantially important ones in terms of the total impact of the teacher on the student.

As a church-related institution, Stetson University has devised an unusual method of screening faculty candidates. A faculty committee in 1951 wrote a statement entitled "What Is a Christian College?" When a candidate applies for a position, the dean sends him a copy of the statement and requests his comments and reactions in as much detail as possible. When the reply comes back, it is assessed not for agreement with the position taken in the statement but for the amount of intelligent criticism reflected in the answer.

Attempts at Training and Evaluation

In our travels we have found, as many before us, that teaching is a preciously guarded profession. On every campus, faculty members stressed the freedom of the teacher. In some cases the concern over freedom had led to a strict individuality. Colleges, for instance, which have attempted to train the inexperienced instructor have run into cries of anguish from the experienced. This, they say, is stereotyping the profession. As one told us, "Each teacher must be free not only to chose what he will teach but how he will teach it." Faculty members for the most part do appear willing, however, to discuss methods and bases for advising and counseling. On some campuses their willingness has been useful as a jumping-off-point for discussion of teaching itself.

With the help of the Danforth Foundation, Stetson University established two years ago an in-service training program for a limited number of faculty with counseling interests. It was designed for a discussion of both personal and academic counseling. The Stetson program calls for ten faculty members from various departments to meet regularly for a year in a continuing discussion of methods and problems. Periodically, outside experts are brought in for a day or a week end of consultation. In June of each year the group meets off campus for a week of intensive review and summary. Faculty interest in the program was shown by the voluntary action of last year's group to continue their meetings for another year. Those with whom we talked who had participated mentioned new depth and significance in their contact with students.

Programs such as this one appear to offer one way to enter the sacred arena of the classroom. Certainly, every institution can profit from better academic, as well as personal, advising. Where full training is impossible, beginning with a nucleus *is* possible.

As another example, at Stephens College the strong emphasis on the individual student has led to the establishment of an in-service training program for faculty advisers. Each faculty member advises from four to twelve students as an integral part of his responsibilities. The typical adviser has eight advisees. In order that the advising may be as helpful as possible, the faculty member is required to participate in the Stephens in-service training program which is supervised by experienced counselors.

First-year faculty members are assigned to small groups which work intensively during the early fall and then once a month all year. The major emphasis in these groups is on the practical aspects of advising, such as sources of referral and information, and general college policy. During the second year of teaching, faculty members meet monthly to discuss counseling techniques and personnel procedures. For teachers with more than two years of experience at Stephens, regular discussions are held on more advanced procedures and particular policies or problems.

The director of the professional counseling service, assisted by experienced teachers, plans and supervises the three phases of this program which are reviewed periodically for weaknesses. An administrative officer told us, "This continuing evaluation is consistent with our basic philosophy that advising should never become haphazard or out of touch with current student needs and interests." A department chairman added, "The fact that the young faculty member has some advisees whose attitudes and problems he knows very well, means that he will not treat a class as though it were a group of sponges to be filled. His enthusiasm for his subject will not be as likely to lead him to forget that there are individuals in this group to whom he is presenting material."

Some institutions attempt through planned programs to make the total business of education a concern of all the faculty. Brooklyn College, for instance, initiated in the fall of 1949 an annual program called Faculty Day. Classes are suspended while faculty participate in discussions related to major problems and concerns of the college. Topics of all kinds are considered in a range extending from student problems to the physical plant. When the subject permits, students are invited to serve as panel members.

Excellence in Teaching

In this chapter we have talked not just about teaching but about good teaching. Excellence in learning flourishes only under the right conditions and with the right people. In its way it makes a contribution of inestimable value to character. The good teacher plays a qualitative role in the educational enterprise.

Unfortunately many of the high goals enunciated here are tempered by reality. There are no easy solutions in a time of increasing enrollments and proportionately diminishing numbers of teachers. The problems grow more and more acute each month and make more difficult the establishment of conditions requisite to effective learning. The small college is beset by the shortage of teachers of quality, and the large university must cope both with this shortage and with the means of relating the student to the teacher. These conditions make it even more crucial, we believe, for the college not to lose sight of the significant impact which the teacher makes upon the student. While the college struggles with new problems, it should not ignore those which continue.

In many ways, teaching is a self-perpetuating profession. Good teachers inspire students to join them; poor teachers discourage. The example of a teacher devoted to his subject and caring intelligently for his student may be the strongest factor in drawing students to the profession of teaching.

In these pages we have attempted to state the qualities of the teacher which, according to our conversations with students and faculty members, affect most profoundly the student. We have tried, in addition, to imply their significance to character development. The good teacher knows and likes his subject together with knowing and liking his student. Beyond this, he devotes himself assiduously to reducing his own ignorance, while never hesitating to make known to the student the commitment in his discipline which he avows. His particular commitment may change. The fact that it might change, however, does not alter his obligation to tell where he stands at the same time that he gives all points of view. The example of a man devoted to learning and with a passionate concern for excellence serves the student well. If, to this, may be added the force of personal conviction, the scene is set both for the higher levels of learning and for the sound development of character.

4. *The Organization of the Curriculum*

> After taking all these courses, I really hope my education is going to add up to something. Right now it's a dab and a dribble. Many of my courses really make sense, and I get excited about them. But others—well, they just don't offer me anything but a few more credits toward the degree. That's the impression I have, I'm sorry to report.

> Students and faculty must not consider themselves to be in opposite corners of an academic boxing ring. They must fight complacency together.

THE FIRST were the words of a student just returned from a class in economics, leaning back in his chair at the Student Union while he sipped a cup of coffee. To his remarks we have added the substance of an editorial in the *Colorado Daily*, the student newspaper at the University of Colorado. Whether over coffee or in print, both sentiments reflect what we found in talking with students and faculty wherever we traveled. In large and small degrees, every campus which we visited conveyed to us some unhappiness over the rigidity of the curriculum, the lasting impact of tradition upon it, and the unwillingness of some to examine realistically the depth of the effect upon the student in preference to the extent of coverage in a particular subject.

The comments of both students and faculty members led us to consider the place of the curricular organization in character development. We found our observations in this area to be the most difficult to assess and the most debatable. Because, however, we believe them to be among the most important in our study, we shall attempt to reflect what the majority of conversations and interviews revealed. Again we turn to a summary of major points of agreement among those with them we talked regarding the particular rationale of the curriculum which apparently is most effective in its impact on the thinking and attitude of the students. In some cases we attended the classes which they identified as significant to them; in others, we presumed to interrupt a student intent on his studies to discover why he found his academic endeavor so stimulating.

The Essential of Student Interest

In reviewing what we found, we conclude first of all that no curricular organization is really successful without the basic ingredient of student interest and enthusiasm. There is no guarantee of profound effect beyond this point, but without student interest it is impossible to stimulate sound learning and reliable scholarship. When a student told us, "I just can't get excited about this course," it meant to us that he would gain little, if anything, beyond the minimum necessary to slide through.

It was interesting to note that freshmen especially were unhappy with the work they were asked to undertake. We are forced to conclude that a surprising number of the colleges we visited fail to recognize fully the importance of the freshman year in gaining and holding student interest in academic work. One might expect that special emphasis would be placed on this all-important initial period in academic life. On the contrary, in many instances freshman courses were the most tradition-bound and the teaching the least inspiring. Unless the student is challenged and becomes, to some degree, fascinated at this point, later efforts to interest him will meet with far less success. A senior noted, for example, "Maybe my hopes about what I'd study in college were too high. But, in the middle of my freshman year, I suddenly discovered that I'd become awfully sour. I was pretty cynical about the great things the college said it was going to do with me. I've recovered somewhat, but that first experience started me off on no feet at all." And a freshman down the hall gave evidence that the process was being repeated when he asked, "Just *what* are they trying to do to me? I don't see any sense to the kind of thing I'm studying."

Several faculty members attempted to put their fingers on the cause of the inadequacy of the freshman year. Some felt that the break between high school and college must be one of substance as well as form. They asserted that some college teachers are not sufficiently well acquainted with the nature and content of secondary education. We found evidence to indicate this was sometimes true. When, for instance, we touched upon secondary education in our faculty interviews, many teachers appeared to be basing their observations on their own high school experience which had run its course often twenty to thirty years previously. As one faculty member commented, "I don't understand why these freshmen have so much trouble adjusting. *We* didn't when my class jumped from high school to college." And another revealed himself when he stated, "I start these students in English Literature where they left off at the end of high school. We begin with *Hamlet*. I'll never forget my senior high school English teacher who said that *Hamlet* should only be read when the reader is 'ready' for it. One loses his appreciation if he reads it too early." The student of thirty years ago, however, may have lacked the sophistication of today's high school youth. Perhaps he wasn't "ready," and perhaps they are. There is reason to believe that substantial changes in the attitudes of youth take place within a decade or more. Young people, for instance, are bound to have felt the impact of the major social changes within the last thirty years. And this is something with which faculty members will do well to reckon.

Another study of freshman attitudes, conducted under the auspices of the Educational Records Bureau, noted that

Requirements are especially onerous if they involve repetition of work done earlier. Even if, in theory, college is a continuation of previous instruction, some freshmen find that their first year work backtracks on ground already covered. Loss of motivation and interest results if this work occupies more than a small part of the time. It is useless to point out to the boy who reports that college French has just forced him to read *Columba* for the third time that language preparation varies greatly in high schools, and that a heterogeneous class has resulted. Boredom may affect all parts of his study.[1]

We have thus identified student interest as the threshold. All else we report in this chapter is related to gaining and holding the interest of students at a level which does not imply the easier expedient of lowering standards or simplifying what is taught. It is a difficult task sometimes to capture student interest and to elicit student enthusiasm, but the obstacles are minor compared with the rewards.

Relating the Subject to the Student

We have not attempted a thorough study of curricular offerings, but on the basis of our conversations we have observed certain factors of significance in gaining the interest of students. The relevancy to the student of the subject matter as presented is one such factor. By relevancy we imply that both the material of the course and the method of presentation are such that they challenge the student to reconsider his own attitudes and values. We found, for example, as one naturally expects, that students study subjects initially because of their particular interests and the contribution which the newly acquired knowledge can add to their lives. Students told us that this was why they enrolled in courses in psychology or biology or mechanical engineering or philosophy, to mention but a few. What significance does this have to the teacher? Obviously, here is a good beginning point. We do not imply that each course must be "student-centered" just to cater to this concern. We believe only that the faculty member might well ask himself as he faces a class: "Why are these students here before me? What brought them here? What do they want me to do with them?" Our conversations have re-

[1] Agatha Townsend, *College Freshmen Speak Out* (New York: Harper & Bros., 1957), pp. 36–37.

vealed repeated instances of student disillusionment with faculty who were said to cover the subject in as sterile a fashion as possible, seldom acknowledging its relationship to those who study it. Perhaps this is the background for the concern of one student who told us, "They keep telling me that college is preparation for life, but I'm alive now."

The absence of relevance has some side effects of importance to those anxious to relate the college experience to the development of character. If the collegiate experience is regarded only as getting ready for something ahead, perhaps the student may come to feel that there are two worlds in which he is permitted to live—the here and the then. Not infrequently we came across the student who was frank enough to admit, "I really don't see any relationship between my cheating now and what I'll do later in life. Because I get my kicks today doesn't mean that I'm always going to be living it up." A corollary is found in the attitude of the increasing number who look upon undergraduate education as a mere step toward the really important experience of postbaccalaureate study. Several institutions which we visited were deeply affected by the emphasis on future graduate work. As one student commented, "We don't really think of these four years as particularly important. The ones ahead offer the real experience."

The professor need not make a direct attack on relating the course to the student in order to achieve the desired goal. In some cases, for instance, it may be accomplished more successfully if the student first studies in broad strokes the nature of man and then applies this knowledge to himself. But this second step, the element of self-application, does not occur automatically. It needs the stimulus of faculty encouragement. Oft-cited examples were the initial and widespread student fascination with psychology which was too frequently killed by a lack of relatedness, or the interest in philosophy which waned because the teacher failed to make clear, as one professor put it, that "Plato is important not just because he had great ideas but because those ideas are important to each individual and to all men." Similarly, although we found few students who read a daily newspaper with regularity, the initial interest they do have in current events goes unchallenged by the French teacher. As one student remarked, "I'd like to be able to understand General De Gaulle's rise to power. It must be related to earlier French crises but you'd never know it from the course I'm taking." In turn, we found several students who stated that they were currently "covering" the Russian revolution of 1917 without even a hint of its significance to the present struggle. Over and over, students with whom we talked suggested that their excitement both for courses and for current events might be increased substantially if some sense of relatedness was offered.

Another fairly popular technique is commonly known as the "shock treatment." A junior described it this way: "Sometimes it happens in a psych or philosophy course when the prof says something that riles you all up and makes you angry. Then the ideas that you've had in the back of your mind, but never really thought much about, come to the front and you begin thinking. You try to decide what it is that makes you angry at what he said. That's when you start to feel maybe you are learning something."

That there are questions in the minds of students is too obvious to need statement. On the basis of our study, however, we think it not too obvious to ask what disciplines really offer the answers, or the beginnings to the answers, to those questions. A dean concluded, "I really don't think it's unreasonable to expect each faculty member in his own way and through his own subject-matter field to contribute to the student's definition both of man and of himself." And an associate professor of physics noted, "We all agree there is order in the universe. We can make that plain to the student in the teaching of math and of the natural sciences, for instance. I do agree that every course has something to offer."

As part of its Core Program, Colgate University has taken one of many possible approaches in the development of a freshman course intended as a major intellectual attack on long-standing prejudices and unexamined attitudes. In our visit to Colgate many of the freshmen as well as upperclassmen with whom we talked singled out the first-year course in Problems in Philosophy and Religion as one of the most important experiences of their academic career thus far. The entire Core Program is described as an attempt to provide "breadth of knowledge as a basis for later specialization, and within that breadth to help the students to see something of the ordered nature and interrelations of the disciplines of human knowledge." Within this broad overview, faculty members claim to work intensively in limited areas, exciting the student by intensive study and discussion which help him realize the nature of the problems faced in each particular field.

The freshman course in philosophy and religion begins with selected readings from various points of view. Among them are Roman Catholicism, Protestantism, scientific naturalism, and communism. Each reading is taught as if it were a complete and final truth. The intent is to capture student thought and then to turn it about in the realization that not everything the professor has taught so fervently can possibly be true. The faculty then emphasize to the students that they may have been unable to reconcile these differing perspectives because they do not yet know enough about the background for these ideas which shape the thinking of men in our society. Therefore, the students must go back and study the sources from which men received these ideas before they will be able to analyze them logically. One faculty member told us, "I think quite a few students come with convictions. Whether these are good or bad, I don't know. We try to open up their minds first and then have them take in the more examined values. Values are not valid unless they are examined."

After the initial provocative section, the class turns to the study of Plato, Aristotle, the Old Testament, and the Jewish concept of history. Then comes the New Testament, followed by the Stoics and Epicureans. Augustine and Aquinas conclude the first semester. During the second term the course moves into the development of modern thought—Luther, Locke, Smith, Hume, and leaders in the nineteenth century. The end of the term is devoted to a review of the positions considered at the outset.

The course is taught by nine men of widely divergent points of view. The staff meets frequently to "battle through" the material to be taught. The chairman told us that the actual assignments are reworked each year and new material sought which will be teachable as well as pertinent to the points the faculty want to stress. Obviously, this course is dependent on the caliber of the teaching. Unless properly and skillfully handled, it might well have a strong negative effect. We found, however, as we have indicated, enthusiastic student response. Students at Colgate and in all the institutions we visited appear to respond well to courses which offer them raw materials for independent thought and action. They seem to prefer that which forces them to ask questions over that which gives them the answers.

Explorations in Depth and Attempts at Synthesis

Wherever we traveled we uncovered honest yearning among both students and faculty members for some intellectual rationale which is not available in the hop-skip-and-jump curriculum so frequently found. Some felt that the best solution lies in greater depth; others were vociferous on the need for relaxing traditional subject-matter boundaries. An Oberlin faculty committee, for example, spoke of "the intrinsic failure which derives from the very nature of the concept of undergraduate specialization: the belief that real understanding may be acquired through study of a field in virtual isolation from other areas of knowledge. The complex of human thoughts and actions, achievements and failures, cannot be compartmentalized without constant danger of superficiality, narrowness, or error." Out of the widespread argument between depth and synthesis will come, we trust, some creative curricular reorganization.

The students with whom we talked appeared to value both approaches, provided certain ingredients are added. In any case, they were heated in their resentment of higher learning offered in small doses of apparently unrelated material. Though many students enjoy the experience of delving deeply and systematically into a particular subject, they still want that subject to reflect a larger usefulness. We found many who complained of the single subject-matter course which is factually organized without apparent relationship to broader principles. Mere assimilation of subject matter, even though it be logically organized and presented, is not enough. A faculty member observed, "It's easy to give just the facts, but to give meaning to the facts is a stretching experience for the teacher long before he joins the class."

Frequently we came across attempts to bridge the gap between and among subjects without going so far as devising entirely new courses. The experimental preceptoral program at the University of New Hampshire, for instance, stems from a concern over the apparent inability of many freshmen students to envisage their educational experience as a "meaningful, integrated whole." This university offers the usual senior synthesis program, but the preceptoral effort has been designed to challenge and stimulate the student from his first days on campus.

At New Hampshire one hundred freshmen are chosen from volunteers to participate in the noncredit experiment. The program is an attempt to supplement and complement the courses in biology, history, and English which are taken concurrently. The students are divided into four groups of twenty-five each. They meet two hours weekly with a faculty preceptor who acts as a discussion leader, guide, and more experienced layman. Preceptors conduct the weekly meetings almost entirely as a discussion. During the first part of the year, before the students have become sufficiently acquainted with the three subject courses, the attempt is made to analyze the general aims and some of the problems of higher education, together with their relevance to the individual. As the year progresses, the students are urged to evaluate the nature and uses of the subjects being studied. Discussion topics in the second semester are designed to draw from the basic courses and to encourage an examination of new learning in the light of the meaning and purpose of life. Special attention is given to the responsibilities of educated men and women.

The New Hampshire program is still in its trial stages. An attempt will be made to compare the participating group with a control group of similar size which followed the usual pattern. We received mixed reaction to the program from both faculty members and students. Whether or not it succeeds, it does give evidence, however, of an honest attempt to break the lock step of the traditional curriculum.

We found experiments in general education to be almost as numerous as the number of colleges concerned with overspecialization. Many were attempting to integrate subject matter through the organization of one or more, or a series of several, cross-disciplinary courses. As one in charge stated, "Our effort is directed toward analysis *with* synthesis." The divisional committee in charge of the Humanistic Tradition course at Oberlin College observed, "The development of interdepartmental, cross-fertilizing courses and programs which challenge students to give historic orientation to all values, to works, systems, and faiths which express them, to explore the precise referents of the terms they use, to analyze, compare, and evaluate all ideals, ideas, and actions is, we feel, a more fruitful lead towards the enlargement and the maturity of the student than the dominant specialization and cross-purposiveness which so often today wastes not only the time of students but also the efforts of teachers."

We found some faculty members who viewed with great trepidation the course or courses which attempt to present the full scope of human achievement. This type of course, they feared, prevents the experience of discipline which one gains only from thorough exploration into a particular area. And, as one added, "Discipline is certainly a necessary part of learning." Not a few faculty members were fearful also lest, in attempting to teach a survey or synthesis course, they lose contact with their own discipline. To this argument came a reply from one who believes ardently in the general education approach: "Faculty may take some assurance that if they are not connected with their particular trade-union, they *will* connect with the student."

We found that many students welcome some opportunity to sense and to examine the totality of knowledge. A senior girl told us, for instance, "I wanted a broad, liberal background, but I found soon that we have to choose a major. I chose sociology just because it was less restrictive and less prescribed than the others. I'm not that enthusiastic about sociology by any means. It was the only way I could manage to study all the things I wanted to. I'd like to find out not just what one area contributes but what all of them add up to." A professor commented, "Man's responsibility to himself is very great indeed, and it requires that his view of all things really be just that, a view of all things—as far as possible, a view of everything." It is this concern which has led college after college to seek new ways to bring together into some logical studying order man's total approach to himself and to his world. We joined one student group which heard a faculty member ask these questions:

Do I insist that what is important is and must be something which is important in the immediate present? Or shall I be willing to consider the past? Do I identify myself simply with my colleagues who are living now, or do I try to sense the whole experience of the wisdom of the race? Am I willing to consider the question of tradition? Do I consider, for instance, the human image simply as I happen to meet it—walking around on the street, God help me—or do I view the human image at all times and in all places and contexts?

Some faculty members mentioned to us also the importance, in making learning more creative, of greater use of original sources to stimulate the student's own synthesis. As one remarked, "I'm afraid we rely too heavily on secondary sources which provide a tailor-made synthesis for the student. This becomes, then, nothing more than studying all over again what somebody else put together. The actual experience of relating and assembling should not be lost."

We pause now to describe some additional examples of efforts to overcome the dangers of fragmentation and specialization. We do not pretend to say that these are the best, or even better than many others, but only that they are ones we found to be highly regarded in their own locales.

1. The University of Wisconsin has a long history of experimentation with programs of integrated study. The present Integrated Liberal Studies (ILS), now in its tenth year, has emerged from many previous ideas and experiments. Designed for freshmen and sophomores, this separate administrative unit of the College of Letters and Science has an enrollment of about three hundred students.

The ILS program offers a general education through a closely knit sequence of courses which, by unity of plan and interrelation of content, aim to make more meaningful and coherent the diverse elements in the usual liberal education. The purpose is to make the subjects studied become significant in relation to each other. Each course, thus specifically created, is required of every student enrolled in the ILS division.

Some of the faculty with whom we talked described this particular undergraduate curriculum as an introduction to Western civilization. The courses cover divisions of knowledge rather than specific subjects. The three divisions are the humanities, the social studies, and the sciences. Courses within a division draw together and integrate materials and techniques from several contributing areas. They follow an historical or a developmental sequence. The divisions are further integrated with one another by cross references in lectures and discussions and through assignments and essays.

With the exception of English Composition, each course consists of a series of lectures by one or more professors followed by periods of discussion. Students are assigned to groups of about twenty members with each group remaining an unbroken unit throughout the semester. One faculty member pointed out that, in this way, "our students enjoy the advantages of a small, compact group within the large university. They study together a compact pattern of courses." Our observation of student life led us to conclude that this association promotes group loyalty and additional group activities of a social as well as of an intellectual nature. ILS at Wisconsin is an interesting example of a small unit operating within the larger whole but a unit with which the individual student may better identify himself.

According to the director, the students enrolled in ILS generally have taken a more active part in campus life beyond the classroom and have been associated with student efforts to advance the best interests of the whole university. This has been done, he told us, far out of proportion to the membership. In addition, ILS students have developed a vigorous extracurricular group of their own. A number of students with whom we talked were enthusiastic about the stimulation in and rewards of the ILS program. Lasting results can be assessed only after a more complete and careful evaluation, but a high degree of group rapport is evident.

2. Oberlin College has established a Humanistic Tradition course which is designed as nondescriptive and value-centered. The attempt has been made to integrate the fine arts, literature, religion, and philosophy. The course explores the problems of how men may test their experiences aesthetically as ends to be enjoyed and morally as bases for choices and action. Those responsible for the course claim that it offers juniors and seniors who enroll "the opportunity and incentive for broadening their perspectives,

comprehension and understanding of the multiple and divergent values which human beings have held across the centuries." It attempts to help the student become more aware of his powers of informed discrimination and judgment and of acceptance or rejection of values.

Oberlin students in the course are assigned weekly readings and attend weekly lectures. The use of different men for different lectures helps to bring before the student particular experts in the fields under discussion. In place of quizzes and examinations, five or six short papers are required each semester. At the close of the second semester, students write an integrative paper on a topic of major interest to them.

3. At the strongly church-centered Saint Mary's College the emphasis is naturally on the Christian tradition. Through an historic approach, the student is introduced to many of the aspects of Christian life and thought. The interdepartmental program, elected by a limited number of upperclass women, is an attempt to provide a unified understanding of the historical development of Christian culture. Institutions and law, art, literature, the liturgy, philosophy, and theology are considered as interrelated aspects of culture. The program is designed to offer "a study of the culture process itself, from its spiritual and theological roots, through its organic historical growth, to its cultural fruits." Faculty members say their aim is to provide the students with an enriched understanding of their religious heritage and a deeper comprehension of the Christian roots of their national culture.

In the first year (junior standing) of the program, the course Christianity and Culture introduces the student to the creation and extension of a unified Christian Europe down to the year 1500. The division of Christendom in the sixteenth century and the consequent secularization of culture up to the present are the concern of the second or senior year courses.

Concurrent with the course in Christianity and Culture, the

Colloquium introduces the student, by means of group discussion, to books and works of art which best reflect the cultural process. These sessions aim to make the students more articulate in the discussion of such Christian classics as the *City of God* and the *Divine Comedy*. In addition, the Colloquium includes more intensive study of subjects falling within the four historic periods covered in the course work.

The program at Saint Mary's is implemented by lecture and discussion methods. During its present experimental period, one professor worked with a small group of students (fourteen in 1957–58) for two years, and guest faculty participated where their qualifications were beneficial. As the number of students participating increases, plans call for other teachers to present different phases and periods cooperatively.

In this program the emphasis stems from religious motivation; however, students claim that much of its value lies in the fact that it teaches not religion per se, but man's history within the context of his Christian development. As one girl observed, "I really enjoy this work. I think I've gained some appreciation of the cultural growth of my faith, and my attempt to practice that faith has more meaning." Other students joined her in asserting that Catholicism had become for them a more conscious and profound experience.

Saint Mary's College, like all Roman Catholic institutions of higher education, requires courses in ethics and moral theology of all Catholic students. Through reasoned argumentation, the attempt is made in these courses to aid the students in the formation of convictions and principles basic to consistently good moral action and in the application of moral principles to complex social problems.

4. Wesleyan University has inaugurated a novel program to provide cross-discipline through faculty contact in office arrangement as well as course responsibility. The program offers the pos-

sibility of integration without lessening the responsibility of each faculty member to his own particular discipline. The Public Affairs Center at Wesleyan University is composed of the faculties of the departments of history, economics, and government. The program of the center aims to integrate the social sciences and to promote teaching and research arising out of the interests of departmental members.

The purpose of the center with its own special facilities is to avoid excessive specialization and departmentalization in the social sciences and to move away from the traditional textbook-lecture instructional methods. It attempts, through seminars involving the use of faculty from two or more of these departments, to interrelate the disciplines and to probe the underlying values in each. Some of the interdepartmental courses which have resulted from the work of the center are: Social Ethics and Public Policy, Economic Development, American Political Theory, and Decision Making in Public Affairs.

The center provides workshops, seminar rooms, classrooms designed for panel discussions and conferences, a statistical laboratory, and a press archives room housing the newspaper clipping service. Students are given the opportunity in workshops to deal with the raw materials, documents, and the data of the social sciences under the supervision of tutors.

Again, student testimony emphasized the value to students of the center. It is far more than the often-found one-shot senior course. Some of the faculty members with whom we talked felt that the success of the center is due to the continuity in the integrative attempt. Others mentioned the strong quality of the student's first-year program as an important basis for the center's effort, as well as effective administrative support and leadership.

These are but a few programs of the many we have observed. Whatever the approach, however, it was evident from our conversations with students that many of them appreciate the trend away from heavy dependence on specialization. The combination of the experience of depth together with some attempt at synthesis or integration appears to offer an especially helpful experience to the student. Both depth and synthesis are important; one without the other is insufficient.

Tradition and the Structure

In a luncheon lecture, the dean of the faculty of one university echoed the concern of many when he observed, "We should get rid of the idea that a student shouldn't be expected to know something unless he's had a course in it. . . . We should work toward greater sense of qualitative rather than quantitative education." The majority of students with whom we talked accepted as inevitable the traditional structure of the curriculum with its emphasis in most colleges on the number of credits earned and on grade averages. Faculty members, however, appeared far less ready to capitulate to a perpetuation of the heavy reliance on artificial criteria. The student dissatisfaction has not yet resulted in a substantial number of experiments. On but a few scattered campuses did we find any genuine movement away from the traditional credit and marking systems. Obviously the successful and satisfying method of evaluation has not been devised.

The comments of students did reveal an unhappy attitude toward what they were learning as merely an accumulation of credits and marks. The possibility of inequality in the system also raised questions in the minds of students. Although he has no desire to see any of his classmates fail to pass a course, the student does question the validity of his own marks when he sees a professor arbitrarily "upgrade" poorer students.

Goddard College, with a student body of less than one hundred, has adapted to its own purposes the attempt to evaluate the person as well as the extent of assimilated knowledge. Before a student may move from his second year into the upper-class courses, his record is scrutinized carefully by the entire faculty. The faculty attempts to determine to what extent the student, through his attitude and conduct in daily affairs, demonstrates that his education has "taken hold" within him. If he fails to perform as the faculty believe an educated person should, he is asked to withdraw regardless of his marks.

Some of the students as well as faculty members on a number of campuses expressed hope for the time when the student may have freedom to pursue interests when they arise rather than being bound to a strict course outline and prescribed curriculum. Because of schedule difficulties, for instance, it was not infrequent for a student to note that he had chosen his courses on the basis of their availability at certain hours. On several campuses, faculty members discussed also the possibility of revising the curricular structure in such a way as to allow the freshmen to pursue their present interests immediately rather than postponing the process until they had completed basic requirements in such subjects as English, biology, and history. Often, for example, a freshman arrives on campus with a particular interest either in general or vocational fields. He wants a business course or he has looked forward to the study of psychology or philosophy. His reasons may be less mature than the faculty wish, but there is no denying his eager interest. But he is prevented from taking these courses at the time when his interest in them is greatest because he has not yet laid "the foundation." As a result, he tolerates the foundation courses pending the day when he can really dig into something he thinks he will like. As one faculty member noted:

> I think these kids have a genuine gripe. When I want to read a particular book, I get it and read it. I don't like to have someone tell me I have to read fifteen other books first in order to understand the one I want to read. Now I don't mean we should carry this too far, but a little indulgence in student interests while they're alive might not hurt. It's conceivable that a junior or senior might gain much more from our traditional freshman course in Western civilization than the green frosh who doesn't have any interest in it.

Relating Campus Activities to the Curriculum

To the student, his academic world is ideologically and structurally divided. On the one hand, on most campuses, there is strong administrative and faculty support of the purely intellectual program reflected in the course work; on the other hand, the out-of-class life proceeds under its own steam with little more than token concern or guidance. Though this may be an invalid generalization in certain circumstances, it reflects the situation on many campuses which we visited. The opportunity for learning beyond the classroom is seldom paid a fraction of the attention which goes into classroom endeavor. Students themselves bemoan the gap. An editorial in a campus newspaper commented, "The college student is a strange creature, with an uncanny ability to compartmentalize his mind." The writer went on to give an example in student government of how to keep "what one learns in class from seeping into what one does outside of class."

Several colleges which we visited do, however, make a conscious attempt to tie in some of the course work with related but essentially noncurricular activities in which the students engage. The curricular program of International Studies at Macalester College, for example, is supplemented by campus activities which promote international understanding. The over-all intent is to give students a general knowledge of world affairs in order to promote intelligent national and world citizenship. The program has not grown by chance but along with the purposeful administrative direction of the college. The emphasis is deepened by the presence on the campus of over forty students from other nations, one of the largest foreign student enrollments among small liberal arts colleges.

Some of the Macalester travel programs which hold the active interest of both faculty members and students are the Student Project for Amity among Nations (SPAN) through which students spend the summer in various parts of the world, and the Mexican Caravan which is a trip through Mexico to acquaint students with another culture and to give those who study Spanish the opportunity to speak it in its natural habitat. Study groups also make trips to Washington, D.C., and to the United Nations. In addition, Macalester holds annual conferences with students and faculty of United College, an affiliated college of the University of Manitoba, in Winnipeg, Canada. The college has a yearly Political Emphasis Week, the topics for which include different phases of state, national, and international political concerns.

All these international activities are supplemented by a strong and active political science department, by the close relationship with foreign students, by informal discussions, and by such symbols as the display of the United Nations flag along with that of the United States (a symbol mentioned frequently and proudly by students with whom we conversed). The influence and able direction of several key faculty members and administrators contribute substantially to the effectiveness of this international emphasis. The enthusiasm and interest of students were evident to us.

The attempt to interrelate curricular and extracurricular work can, of course, be overdone. The residential campus does provide, however, a natural laboratory for effective testing of some of the ideas and approaches advocated in the classroom.

Direct Contact with the Faculty

A point on which there was unanimous agreement, and which is an integral part of any curricular organization, is that opportunity should be provided for students to deal directly and personally with faculty members. The lack of this opportunity is frequently cited as a criticism of the larger universities. We were interested to find, therefore, that some small colleges are as impersonal in many respects as the largest universities. We conclude that the extent to which the student comes into direct contact with the professor depends more upon the attitude and efforts of the institution than upon its size. We found in talking with students that, through personal contact, students gain a greater sense of involvement and participation in their own education. It is not something which can be stimulated by artificial devices. It results, instead, from a total attitude and approach. In chapter 7 we will discuss this factor in greater detail.

If the curricular organization hinges in large part on the lecture system, little chance is given the student to identify himself with anything more than the cold bare facts. And students on all campuses indicated to us that cold bare facts constitute a sterile form of education. The effort, we believe, must be more than a mere attempt to keep down the size of classes. It is not enough to take pride in the fact that "no class on this campus has more than twenty-five students enrolled." This appears to guarantee nothing except that large classrooms are unnecessary.

We turn to Radcliffe College as one example among many of an effort to use more effectively the smaller class. Any explanation of the academic program at Radcliffe must first establish that academic instruction for Radcliffe girls is the legal responsibility of the Harvard College faculty and that all Harvard and Radcliffe students are taught together in classes. In essence, Radcliffe students are receiving a Harvard education in the Harvard tradition which relies strongly on the tutorial method. Radcliffe honors candidates (about 50 percent of the enrollment) participate in departmental tutorials in their field of concentration, with the exception of those majoring in a science or music. The precise form and extent of the tutorials vary according to departments. Some require two years; others offer three. In some of the large departments, small group tutorials are held, but all students still work individually with a tutor on thesis preparation.

Most of those with whom we talked agreed that this opportunity for individual work and discussion, with the tutor's help in correlating courses and in stimulating wide reading and scholarly methods, is essential to an invigorating intellectual experience. Plans now under way call for an extension of the amount of work done with tutors. In spite of the excellence of many of the lectures, we found many Radcliffe students pointing to the tutorials as the initial focus of stimulation.

Curriculum and Character Influences

In this chapter we have attempted to explore some of the patterns of curricular organization which appear to influence the character growth of the student as well as to offer to him the opportunity to develop directly those principles which will give intelligent direction and purposeful control to his life.[2] The greatest impact on character occurs, we believe, as a result of the total campus experience. One important facet of this experience, the curriculum and its particular mode of operation and organization, cannot be ignored by those who seek to promote character influences. The curriculum is the fundamental structure within which the principal task of education takes place. The college is dependent in no small part on its course offerings in its attempt to fulfill its responsibility for the character education of its students. We have concluded, therefore, that the effective curricular organization must capture and hold student interest; that it must provide opportunity for depth study as well as synthesis; that it should attempt a break from the overemphasis on tradition in its structure; that it might well furnish some effective bridge between the curricular and extracurricular experiences of the stu-

---

[2] The Association of Higher Education is sponsoring a study, directed by Dr. Marjorie Carpenter, which aims to gather information demonstrating that in regular subject-matter courses of the curriculum there can be a conscious and rewarding attention to the values involved. There are faculty members who encourage students to articulate and re-examine their own values in such disparate courses as biology, social studies, literature, and psychology. Dr. Carpenter's material will be examined by Dr. Huston Smith who will endeavor to reach some conclusions on the basis of the evidence presented. Because of this concurrent study, we have not attempted here to deal in detail with approaches of this nature.

dent; and that, no matter what the subject, there should be evident some apparent relationship to principles. In this way, we believe the college can contribute through its curriculum most effectively to the experience of disciplined enlargement of knowledge which, in itself, is an important part of character growth.

5. *The Degree of Student Responsibility*

I'm not one for a lot of this gobbledygook. We shouldn't always be pampering and building up the students. After all, life won't. Let's be truthful with them. Don't tell them they have free rein, when you know very well you'll have to check them many times. Students see through people easily—and the people who work with them are a mighty important influence. We have to develop a combination of ease, cooperation, and respect.

IN EVERY DISCUSSION touching on concepts of character, we heard the word "responsibility" mentioned so often that we concluded this was one area deserving special observation. There were those, for instance, who were content with defining character as the responsibility one assumes for himself and for others. Though this definition would not satisfy all, some element of self-development is included in every approach to education. What role should the college play? What are its limits? What are the benefits to be derived? These are questions which we will attempt to answer as we explore the degree of student responsibility, actual and potential.

In talking with administrative officers and faculty members, we found a wide range of views regarding the extent to which students should be given responsibility. The question basically is to what degree the college can afford to become democratic. How can it maintain its own continuing identity and yet give its transient students experience in making decisions and assuming responsibility? In reply, some presuppose a relationship of the experienced to the inexperienced. One dean commented, for instance:

I don't believe in students having too much responsibility in setting the pace, mores, standards, or policies of an institution of higher learning. The student comes to the institution and pays for what we as specialists have to offer him. We represent, academicians and administrators together, the stewardship of our special fields and areas. I propose a system whereby we use our decision-making processes as teaching tools, allowing students the opportunity to observe, criticize, and question, but not actually to exert direct control. The element of "let's pretend" has some value as a way of teaching. Let's realize the difference between pretending and acting through demonstration techniques as the forerunner of the real thing.

Those who hold this view believe that the college is the source rather than the scene of actual experience. As one president stated, "Students should be encouraged to provide information, opinions, reactions, and, indeed, wise suggestions. But I should not suppose them to be the chief source of values the university wishes to live by. Otherwise, we repudiate our own leadership, our experience, and the efficacy of the education which we proudly acclaim."

Some faculty members take a more extreme position in their reaction to any student participation. They feel that students abuse freedom and shirk responsibility. We found in talking with them, however, that often they based their views on disillusioning personal experiences with a group of students somewhere back along the line. They appeared to fail to appreciate that every four years a completely new set of students occupies the campus. And, furthermore, these are students who have not had the opportunity to learn from previous success and failure.

Others take a different stand. Some indicated that the degree was a matter of guided responsibility. As a chairman of a faculty committee on student activities noted, "I think people are trying to give students a good amount of responsibility around here. They aren't attempting to fool the students, however, by saying that they are running the institution. We let them into pretty high levels, but we also let the students know that the final authority still rests with us."

Finally, some hold that the student should be a fully participating member of the academic community. He should be held responsible only for those standards and policies which he or his representatives have helped to establish. On a few campuses which we visited this meant almost complete student participation in all of the decisions of the campus community. The range extended from admission policies to parking regulations.[1]

Regardless of administrative and faculty opinion, however, students on all the campuses we visited talked about wanting greater freedom and more responsibility. In one institution in particular there had been heated arguments over rules and regulations, particularly in the social arena. Threatened with more stringent social restrictions, a junior girl wrote a letter to the editor of her campus newspaper protesting that students want to be something besides machines. In bitter language she said,

> It is time to herald the Thinking Machine. No emotion, no benefit of experience—just an enormous brain—reading, listening to scholars, writing papers, taking exams. Learning about democratic ideology, but not having the terrible conflict of acting. And if the machine lasts four years without breaking apart or running down [it will be given] a piece of paper and [made into] a man or woman, prepared to assume its role in a much less bright society.

Though seldom as bitter, many students expressed to us an honest desire to assume greater responsibility in both academic life and campus living. Each college, it would appear, must work out its own rationale and degree.

The Principle of Participation

Properly given and properly assumed, participation offers an important lesson to the college student. From our observations we would conclude that the student who is involved in his own education is apt to develop a far deeper sense of actual responsibility for himself and for others than the one who is merely held

[1] The question of student participation is explored in full in Harry H. Lunn, Jr., *The Student's Role in College Policy-Making* (Washington: American Council on Education, 1957).

responsible. His involvement should include not only campus life in the extracurricular and governing areas, but also his entire academic experience. The student is faced with a confusing sense of values when one part of his college stresses independence while the other denies it. If he does not become involved in the classroom, for instance, he feels no special responsibility to participate even in his own learning process. He is then simply being subjected to the experience of education, an experience not likely to have much meaning or value. We were particularly impressed, therefore, by the colleges which are able to strike the balance in both curricular and extracurricular areas. In these colleges we sensed that the students were really participating in a partnership in everything they did. Because, too, they felt greater responsibility for themselves, they appeared to us to assume greater responsibility for others.

Participation offers also no small side benefits. We found that the participating student becomes sufficiently involved in the life of the academic community to gain a far better understanding of the function of that community and the role it plays in the world around it. He senses why institutions of higher learning exist and what constitutes both their contribution to and responsibility for society. An editorial in the *Cornell Daily Sun* reflected the sentiments of many with whom we talked. In part it stated:

> If the University wishes to take the view that its students are not mature enough to make value judgments as to what is morally correct and what is not, then it must realize that it is negating one of its basic educational premises. For the most part, students are mature enough to see that they have certain responsibilities at the University and must conduct themselves in a certain manner; if they are not, they do not belong here. University life is a period of maturing; if the conditions for maturing are not offered to the students, they will be unable to do anything except conform to the [minimum] code which has been set for them.

We sensed also that participation serves the additional useful purpose of pulling the student away from lesser allegiances to a larger loyalty. If he engages in activities of importance to the larger community, he is bound to sense a responsibility for that community. It was surprising to us, therefore, to find several colleges which, with seeming indifference, allowed students to pledge their interests to smaller units within the institution. Such units exist on every campus, regardless of the size. They range from informal cliques to such highly organized and influential living units as fraternities and sororities.

Responsibility in the Classroom

If, as we have said, responsibility is to be offered the student any place on the campus, evidently it should begin in his academic experience. The teacher should recognize at the outset that not all new students are fully prepared to assume responsibility. Their lack of experience and their attitude may stand in the way at the beginning. A faculty member commented, "It takes me almost a term to get these freshmen to recognize that I'm not going to check up on every assignment. They expect and even want me to at first. Then they begin slowly to realize that they'll get out of my courses exactly and only what they themselves want." Initial difficulties with students should not be taken, therefore, as justification by the faculty member of practices which serve only to smother the potentiality of awakening the student's sense of responsibility. We came across a number of students, for instance, who complained rather bitterly about exclusive dependence on objective examinations, on rigid attendance rules, and on other practices which students view as paternalism.

A number of colleges and universities continue to experiment with programs for the student who has proven his ability as well as sense of responsibility. Most of the ones we observed emphasize independent study with the superior student given maximum opportunity to set his own limits. Some colleges, for instance, allow the above-average upper-class student to replace one or two regular courses with individualized work. Others permit the student to free himself entirely of the formally organized curriculum. In this approach, there is, of course, some danger of isolating the student from the give-and-take with others in the classroom atmosphere. Independent study, we believe, is best combined, therefore, with group work.

Both faculty members and students indicated to us the high esteem in which they hold certain of these so-called honors programs. One professor, in describing his own program, stated, "Questioning and interest in intellectual pursuits should start way back, and one must have basic information to work with. Then add an interested, excited faculty, and lots of independent reading and writing." On another campus a student added, "Honors courses are the most productive experience on campus—they push you to do your own thinking. When it comes right down to it, truly independent study is one of the best ways to learn." Programs emphasizing the individual do tax the collegiate budget. The college engaging in extensive work of this nature may have to pay the price of emphasis on the individual by curtailing another program or interest if additional funds are not available.

Several institutions which we visited have devised some type of cross-discipline, independent-study program. One such example is the Directed Study program at Denison University which is essentially a junior course in independent study, leading to honors work in the senior year. Participating students do independent research and writing of a nature and extent prescribed by the particular department with which they are working. At Stetson University a growing Honors Studies program combines independent research and writing in several related subjects with group discussion on each individual's findings. Radcliffe students participate in the tutorial method of Harvard which has already been mentioned.

The Honors College at Wesleyan University provides the opportunity for students of superior standing to engage in individual programs of study under the direction of faculty tutors. The purpose, according to the Wesleyan description, "is to bring together the best students in various fields to give them opportunities to become acquainted with each other and to hear and engage in discussion with distinguished men in one or another field. The extent to which the Honors College fulfills its function depends entirely on the individual student and the depth and vitality of his desire to participate in its activities and to profit by them."

Normally, Wesleyan honor students pursue the special course in the senior year, but in unusual cases the committee does admit students during the junior year. A student selects the faculty member or members under whom he wishes to pursue his work. After planning with his tutor a program for the following year, the student submits an application to the Honors Committee for approval. If approved, he works under the direction of his faculty tutor, with whom he has conferences and to whom he submits progress reports.

A member of the Wesleyan Honors College regularly pursues a "distinction tutorial course" and prepares a thesis or a series of reports. The distinction course may include part or all of a regularly scheduled course but it is usually independent study involving laboratory research, library research, or area reading. With the approval of the tutor and the Committee on Distinction, the thesis may take the form of creative work in literature, music, or the fine arts. The student is expected to maintain high standing in general scholarship during the period of his honors candidacy.

One of the earliest, most ambitious, and most comprehensive honors programs in a state university is found at the University of Colorado. Professor Joseph W. Cohen, its director, is now on leave to establish a University Honors Information Service, supported by a grant from the Carnegie Corporation. The service will attempt to "promote and coordinate efforts to solve the national problem of educating the superior student in state-supported universities and colleges" through the collection and dissemination of information on current programs of this kind.

Approximately 8 percent of the students of the College of Arts and Science at Colorado participate in the various honors offerings. One interesting feature of the program is the requirement for participation. High grades do not guarantee acceptance, nor do medium-range marks prohibit application. Each semester the faculty are invited to recommend students who, in their opinion, have the ability and interest to undertake independent and intensive study. In addition, students may themselves apply. They are accepted on proof of sincere interest and willingness to cooperate.

There are three main divisions of honors work. One area is concerned with departmental honors in which students pursuing the same majors work together in small groups. In general honors, the group interests are more varied, and students work in areas outside their major field of concentration, in an attempt to broaden their intellectual understanding. Literature majors, for example, may participate in physical science discussion groups. Each small group has its own method of operation. The general pattern has been to emphasize individual reading and writing, with weekly discussions to stimulate new ideas and give opportunity for experience in groups in confronting ideas through the spoken word. One of the offerings, Junior and Senior Colloquia, is more selective. A small group of the most promising honor students from each class work even more intensively with two selected faculty members.

Historically, the Colorado program has been predominantly an upper-class venture; recently, however, freshmen with records indicating promise have been invited to participate. In addition, the present acting director of honors is working with an experimental high school group in a nearby community.

Many of the faculty members as well as students with whom

we talked indicated a deep interest in extending the methods of such approaches as these to the entire curricular experience and to all students, regardless of ability. The faculty interest stems in part from the surprising discovery that many of the techniques which work well with honors students work equally well with large classes of less-gifted students. A second and perhaps more significant reason is the increasing conviction among many that the challenge to deepen perspective should be made early in the student's career before the specialization of upper-division work and the demands of campus activities consume his time and interests. An adaptation such as this would mean a revolution in the traditional structure of curricular life. One faculty member noted, however, "The college errs too often on the side of tradition by holding to the rigidity of class schedules, examination and marking systems, and all these prescribed programs of instruction."

It was obvious to us that more experimentation is needed to capitalize on the college's obligation to train the responsible student. The student, we believe, gains a sense of responsibility through experience. The opportunity should be available not just in extracurricular life but through a variety of approaches to study in the curriculum.

The Honor System in Action

Not to be confused with honor programs are the honor systems operating in many institutions. They are similar in their dependence on and encouragement of student responsibility but are related to behavior rather than enlargement of knowledge. In a few of the institutions which we visited, the honor systems cover all phases of campus living from unproctored examinations to dormitory regulations. On most campuses, however, the system operates only at examination time within the confines of the examination room. Some colleges extend the responsibility to placing the student on his honor in outside preparation, such as themes and term papers. Wesleyan University, for instance, allows the student the privilege of taking his examinations back to his dormitory or fraternity room to complete. Oberlin College maintains an honor code which applies to all phases of academic work.

We observed at the United States Naval Academy an interesting example of an honor concept as well as a system. The officers of the Academy subscribe to the belief that honor need not be defined in order to be expected. As a result, no code as such is used. Honor is looked upon as an all-pervading belief in personal integrity as a fundamental attribute of character. It is, therefore, a deeply rooted conviction governing all acts and speech. The unwritten law places all responsibility regarding the definition of right and wrong conduct on each individual and his conscience.

The Academy's honor system is administered by the respective class honor committees and by the brigade (student body) executive committee. The committees are elected by the midshipmen at the start of each year and have the authority to investigate any charge brought before them as well as to make recommendations for punishment. No punitive authority rests with the committees since this is, by regulation, vested only in the Commandant of the Academy.

Coupled with the honor concept is the responsibility given the midshipmen for the operation of their own brigade. Midshipmen are selected for various positions paralleling those of the cadre (the officers). In these capacities they are called upon to make decisions often involving problems of an ethical and moral nature affecting those under their command. The practical application gives focus to the unwritten concept of honor. The Academy makes a direct attempt to place students exemplifying high attributes in the positions of leadership.

The Academy program must, of course, be viewed in the full perspective of the purpose and nature of the military establishment. Faculty members with whom we talked praised the amount of academic honesty; the midshipmen appeared to prize the concept. Frequently in our conversations midshipmen selected for mention certain upperclassmen who, in their opinion, illustrated best the concept. The honor idea was thus personalized.

Brigham Young University has turned its disciplinary procedure into an interesting and apparently successful emphasis on helping the offender recognize the moral consequences of his error, as well as emphasizing the group's responsibility for the individual's misconduct. The honor system operates through two honor councils—the student group which handles typical student cases, and a combined student-faculty council which assumes responsibility for those cases referred to it by the student group as too involved or too serious for a student group to handle alone.

The unusual aspect of the student council is that it does not hand down punitive measures for violations of good conduct and taste. A student who has erred is not viewed as a criminal. Instead he is felt to lack an adequate understanding of the ethical and moral implications of his actions and of the effect they may have on his future life. Each student is counseled by his fellow students on the honor council in the hope that he will recognize the violation of ethics involved and the possible consequences. If attempts at counseling fail, the violator is then referred to the faculty committee for possible punitive action. The majority of cases so handled involve chronic offenders.

We sensed that students at Brigham Young under this system felt more responsible for the conduct of others and were less hesitant about reporting violations. They appeared to realize that any student so reported would not be punished automatically. Instead a sincere attempt would be made to help him overcome his apparent weakness. This approach succeeds somewhat in overcoming the usual barrier in the reluctance to report one's friends.

Both students and faculty members expressed to us deep respect for and pride in the operation of their honor system. Brigham

Young is, of course, a homogeneous community composed almost entirely (96 percent) of members of the Church of Jesus Christ of the Latter Day Saints. Its honor system is, therefore, indigenous. It is built on the foundation of the particular aims and expectations of the university. A program such as this, established from within and in keeping with the purposes of the institution, appears to have a better chance of surviving and of operating effectively.

The university is attempting to organize an orientation program which will provide even more solid support for the honor concept by helping students understand the underlying Christian principles. A faculty member explained to us that the intent is to "point out [to the freshmen] that in some cases this may mean changing some fundamental ways of behavior. For example, one of the highest loyalties one has in high school is loyalty to one's peer group or gang. We want to show them that they are their brother's keeper and that, if they permit him to perpetuate wrong principles, they are doing a disservice to him, to others with whom he comes in contact, to Brigham Young University, and to the church which he represents."

Our observations and conversations have resulted in some general conclusions regarding the success as well as the weaknesses of honor systems. Five factors appear to us to be important in the initial establishment and then the continuing support of the successful system.

First and most obvious is a belief in the basic personal integrity of the student. We find that both faculty and students must assume that the student will not cheat when the conditions make him the responsible person. Second, tied into the faith in personal integrity is the acceptance of responsibility for one's own actions. A student commented, "We all do our best when we really believe that somebody has faith in us. It's the indifference that makes rationalization so much easier." Both the student and the faculty member, therefore, must be willing to commit themselves to the principles of self-responsibility and integrity.

The third factor is perhaps the most troublesome in practice—that of accompanying responsibility for others. The most frequently heard argument against honor systems on campuses where no system operates is that "the student just isn't willing to inform on his fellow students." This becomes most vivid when the fellow student is a roommate, a fraternity brother, a sorority sister, or a close friend. On campus after campus we came across the contention, "Of course I wouldn't squeal on a good friend or a member of my house. It's his business if he wants to cheat, and I'd be a fool to put him on the spot. It's easier when you don't know the person too well." As a result, not a few campuses have given up the attempt to establish an honor system. Students, however, should not be condemned too quickly for such a reaction; certainly it is common among men and women in all society. As a faculty member noted, "I don't blame these students. After all, the faculty themselves aren't really willing to report other faculty. They may talk about somebody cutting corners but they don't march to the president. And yet aren't faculty members under an honor system of sorts?"

The problem is an interesting conflict between the values of honor and of friendship. Which has the higher priority? Neither faculty members nor students have many suggestions for solutions. We have observed, however, some conditions under which the problem is minimized, though never completely solved. On those campuses, such as Brigham Young University, where there is a recognition of the unfortunate effect on the student of his dishonesty, other students are more ready to help. When the student hesitates to talk to the professor or the student committee, he may take the more direct course of speaking personally to the offender or indirectly to him through a mutual friend. He acts to help another, not to report him. Occasionally, too, one finds an institutional ideal placing honor above friendship. If it is vivid enough, students translate it into action. But society impinges on the college. Its own conflicts in priority make the institutional task far more difficult and much less clear.

The fourth factor assumes an attitude toward learning which places the assimilation of knowledge above the drive for grades, credits, and the degree for the degree's sake. Ideally, if the college presents to the student a sufficient challenge and a goal of knowledge toward which he can aspire, external discipline is not necessary. All of the student's efforts will be directed to the acquisition of knowledge. This, however, assumes a common campus dedication which is difficult to achieve and maintain. A student told us, "If it weren't for the necessity of getting good marks in order to get into graduate school, I wouldn't cheat. But the dedication to scholarship around here includes dedication also to a straight A record. Sometimes, you know, one gets in the way of the other."

Finally, the successful system is usually a code or concept which is transmitted chiefly by personal means from one student generation to the next. The students themselves are the purveyors of the tradition. Neither the faculty nor the written statement is as important as what the senior tells the freshman. The idea of honor is communicated from generation to generation as an expectancy and a responsibility which all take pride in assuming. College size need be no determinant of the potentiality of an honor system; we found that it is possible under the right conditions to establish and maintain one in the larger university as well as the small college. Usually a beginning is made in a particular unit of the larger institution from which the concept spreads sometimes to encompass the entire university.

We conclude further that a negation of one or more of the five factors discussed above usually accounts for the failure of honor systems. There may be lacking, for instance, a faith in personal integrity. As one student pointed out, "We got the clue as soon as the prof told us he was going to stay in the room dur-

ing the exam 'just in case somebody is ill.' That not only of-
fended our dignity but taxed our sense of humor." The occasional disillusioning experience may lead both students and
faculty members to question the validity of their faith in personal integrity. And when values conflict and when "informing"
is viewed as the job of someone else, or when friendship takes
precedence over responsibility for others, the system is weakened
and soon becomes unworkable.

Criticisms of the Method

We came across unusually strong criticism of certain classroom
methods as sources of interference both with the honor systems
and as discouragement to the assumption of responsibility. Students claimed that particular methodological practices tempt
them away from commitment to the principles involved. They
cited, for instance, the overemphasis on marks or a heavy stress
on the use of the curve in determining grades. As one student
commented, "We don't mind competing, but this is encouraging
unhealthy competition. And then it often ends up this way: instead of competing with one another, we all gang up and com-
pete with the professor." The result may also be an attitude of
resignation. More than one student has admitted to us, "I don't
bother much any more. We've got one genius in our class, and
the prof never gives more than one A. I'm usually smart enough
to fall into the B bracket, and that's where I'm content to stay."

Students are unhappy (and thus, we believe, lose a sense of
responsibility) when the teacher depends exclusively on objective-
type examinations. The most valuable use of objective tests is to
analyze weaknesses and find the degree to which a student has
acquired background material for more involved thinking. But
if no attempt is made to take the second step, that of testing for
more searching thought, then the student feels that the teacher is
really insulting his intelligence. The student takes the attitude
that the objective test is designed to catch him in his ignorance

rather than to encourage him to integrate and relate what he has learned. Students for the most part appear to us to be fairly perceptive. When they sense that the professor is interested in them only to the extent of obtaining the easy answer, devoid of analysis and simple to correct, they feel no great obligation to respond as individuals. A student described this situation as "a cat-and-mouse game." She said, "He tries to catch us in small errors. Well, we accept the challenge. We outwit him by devising neat little methods of our own so that hardly anybody gets caught. The signals are passed. Of course each one of us manages to put down a few wrong answers so he'll never find out what we're doing."

An editorial in the *Colorado Daily* discussed the question of whether or not the college graduate learns how to think and to weigh various concepts. The editorial stated, "In too many cases, the answer is no. Four years in college may simply signify that one is more adept than most at surviving the multiple-choice, true-false exams which are given in most classrooms. Colleges are turning out satisfied men with empty heads—and it is the colleges themselves which are primarily guilty." We doubt that the situation is that extreme and that simple and that the students are quite so blameless. Nevertheless, when there is no encouragement in method to the student to accept responsibility, he is not likely to devise his own stimulus.

Acceptance of Responsibility

Beyond the classroom, every campus offers opportunity in some form for acceptance of responsibility by the student. A number of organizations and programs aim to stimulate healthy self-concern and personal as well as group reliability. The most obvious examples are the omnipresent forms of student government. On approximately half of the campuses we visited, the governing body or bodies assumed genuine authority and initiative. Nationally, the United States National Student Association is giving active and valuable assistance in stimulating imaginative and organizationally sound activities. On some of the campuses, however, the student government mechanism either has never accelerated or has been devoid of power from the beginning. Many students with whom we talked were as critical of the student government as were the faculty members and administrative officers. One student leader put his finger on a situation which we found repeated on other campuses when he said, "The trouble is that student groups get so upset with wanting to maintain their freedom in little tiny areas. They waste all their energies doing small, unimportant things. When the big ones come along they are by-passed or forgotten. Either the faculty are sick of hearing the students squawk or the students are too busy with trivia to see the possibilities."

A further difficulty was emphasized by a dean of men when he commented, "Students are transient phenomena. The ones who make the decisions are never around to reap the consequences of their acts. As a result, they don't always see the picture in its broad perspective. They want something done immediately and done in a certain way without realizing that another group three years hence may not want it that way. Then *we* have to do the undoing." Occasionally an approach such as this lends itself also to easy administrative rationalization. Where a student government is sound, we have observed that it invariably rests on a solid foundation of mutual respect and trust, usually built upon an even more basic foundation of personal contact between administrators or faculty members and the student leaders.

In addition to the governing organizations on most campuses and sometimes integral to them, there are many forms of student courts and other judicial bodies that handle cases ranging from social misdemeanors to academic infringements. Cornell University has initiated a dormitory judicial system for its male students which has brought the review of infractions into each living unit in order to make judgment as well as a sense of responsibility more personal and relevant. Denison University has a comprehensive judicial system with powers extending to recommendations for expulsion or suspension from the university. With but one exception with unusual overtones known only to the faculty review group, all student decisions have been approved.

Properly established and supported, student judicial work offers a difficult challenge and a rewarding experience to the students involved. We noted with interest that faculty members on many campuses reported that student courts tend to be more strict and to mete out heavier punishments than do faculty committees. For this reason several colleges reported that faculty members like to retain a check on student decisions. Through the experience of making decisions and assessing their own behavior patterns, students are likely to take a more realistic view of the obligations of community life.

We found also frequent instances of attempts to involve students in policy-making and procedural evaluation by bringing together faculty and student leaders in frank and open discussion. Some of these programs are regularly scheduled and some even formally organized. The University of Wisconsin, for example, has a bi-weekly President's Exchange during which the president of the university and the heads of the major student organizations discuss items of current interest to the campus community. We attended one of these sessions and were impressed by the frank discussion. Along with the students, we were also impressed by the fact that the busy head of such a large institution put priority on his contact with students and made certain that he missed as few meetings as possible. On the campus of Brigham Young University the student personnel deans and student leaders meet in a similarly valuable policy discussion session. It was obvious to us that adequate communication among all elements of the college community is essential to continuing assumption of responsibility.

Frequently on many campuses temporary committees are established to deal with particular problems or special crises. We found the Self-Responsibility Committee at Saint Mary's College to be a vigorous example. It had been formed out of the desire to deepen the student sense of responsibility for all areas of college life. The committee at the outset realistically limited itself to one area with which it felt it might cope concretely. It avoided the frequent mistake of attempting to deal superficially with many trouble spots.

During the early part of the college year at Saint Mary's, a trial period was set for the stimulation of more conscious attention to dress, manners, courtesy, and consideration of others. In connection with the latter point, the students noted particular difficulty in the enforcement of "quiet hours" for study purposes in the dormitories. The test period was evaluated by the students and followed by an all-college convocation during which the results were examined and further procedures discussed by the group. As a result of this meeting, the committee established a more realistic system of quiet *areas* rather than hours. We have noted the same decision reached on several other campuses, an indication that students live more by place than by time.

The Saint Mary's committee experiment appeared to provide the freedom requested by the students. It also gave recognition to their growing maturity and ability to deal with their own problems. The program is still in the experimental stage. Thus far it is a good example of the amount of time and care students will devote to governing their own actions if they are given the actual responsibility.

ISSUES OF CONSEQUENCE

Actual responsibility is more than token involvement. One faculty member told us of the difficulties on his campus in getting

other faculty to sense that students could be the responsible parties. We attended with him a meeting of a faculty committee on
student life. The discussion was heated. Two months previously,
the committee had asked a student group for suggestions on how
to handle the problem of infirmary excuses for those who were
genuinely ill. Evidently some students had abused the previous
system, and the infirmary doctors were protesting the rule which
required them to write out a long form for each student with
the sniffles. The student group had presented a plan to the faculty committee which was now viewing it with dismay. One professor observed, "That's the trouble when you ask these kids to
come up with a suggestion. You're honor-bound to consider it,
and it's usually preposterous." The committee debated the issue
at length, with a few holding out, against great odds, for more
student participation. After extended discussion, the minority
voiced the opinion that the student group had been asked only
to make a suggestion, not a decision, and in a limited area devoid
of any real significance. Furthermore, the problem was actually
a trivial one. One of the minority proposed that the group hand
over to the students the entire issue of class attendance and that
it agree to give any student proposal a trial. At the end of the
afternoon the committee concurred.

During a later visit to this same campus we found that the students had accepted the challenge, labored long and hard, and
that the eventual proposal was now the effective system—much
to the surprise of both the faculty committee and, we might add,
the student group.

Here is but one example which led us to conclude that, if
student participation is to be effective, real issues must be involved. We believe that students will respond when they are con-
fronted with vital issues which require them to make decisions
with apparent consequences. They sense immediately when participation is merely tacit representation.

At the University of New Hampshire we found an interesting

approach to joint assumption of responsibility in dealing with a specific problem. Like many colleges and universities throughout the country, New Hampshire had been faced within recent years with a gradual but obvious increase in the amount of alcoholic beverages consumed by students. The increased consumption appeared to be accompanied by an increase in general campus misbehavior and rowdyism. The university administration was faced with two possible courses of action: (1) An outright ban on campus drinking, which appeared to be unworkable and might serve only to create more difficult problems of control; or (2) The stimulation of greater student awareness of the problem and of responsibility for self and group control. The latter course appeared to be the better starting point.

Prior to the opening of the academic year, the administrative officers invited a group of fifty student leaders, faculty members, and civic leaders in the university town to a week-end conference. The purpose was to consider jointly the situation as it existed, possible solutions to the problem, and the delineation of the responsibility of each of the groups represented. The discussion centered around the following questions: (1) Should standards of behavior in a university community vary from those in other communities? (2) Should enforcement and penalties vary? (3) What is the university's responsibility to its public: parents, townspeople, state residents, and so on? (4) Who should assume responsibility for setting standards? What are the relative roles of the administration, student governing groups, the student personnel division, campus police, individual students, and the like? (5) Should the university have a fixed policy? (6) What can individuals do? And (7) what action should we expect from organized groups?

In attending the conference, we observed an improved awareness on the part of the various groups represented regarding the difficulties faced in reaching an adequate solution, the responsibility of each of the various elements in the university community, and the common responsibility of all. Specific suggestions were made regarding action to be taken. As a result of the conference, the university adopted a new policy of more stringent disciplinary measures for those who infringed on the rights of others. Thus far, individual students and student groups have accepted the responsibility of self-control which was agreed upon. It may be too soon to tell, however, whether, because of threat, this is merely a temporary lull or whether a permanent awareness has emerged.

One of the more harassing problems for the continuing faculty member and administrator is that the transient student population often forces them to repeat over and over again such methods as that employed at New Hampshire—at least until the concept of behavior becomes an unwritten tradition communicated from one student generation to the next.

Pasadena City College has attempted to deepen the sense of student responsibility in a continuing program of training for student leaders which emphasizes both the larger aspects and the significance of particular positions. The college sponsors a one-credit course, meeting twice weekly, for elected and appointed student officers. The officers are strongly counseled to take the course, and any other interested students may also participate in it.

Entitled Leadership Principles and Procedures, the course attempts to combine theory and practice in a learning atmosphere. One hour a week is devoted to regular meetings of the student government, with the president of the Associated Student Body presiding and with faculty advisers present but participating only in their advisory capacity. Another hour a week provides classroom instruction in leadership principles, governmental organization, parliamentary procedure, activity development and evaluation, and the responsibilities and ethics of leadership. The individual's experience as a member of student government is used for illustration and evaluation in this second hour. The over-all aim of the course, however, is to develop a basically sound appreciation of the responsibilities of any leadership position.

The course operates in the usual manner of lecture, discussion, and examination. Faculty members told us that the degree and maturity of student participation have increased as a result of the course. To us it seemed that participation in activities at Pasadena was remarkably high for a nonresidential community college. Urban institutions of this type find great difficulty in allotting time for commuting students to hold activity meetings. The absence of resident students reduces the possibility of effective campus activity and governing programs. The Pasadena course for student leaders appeared, however, to give greater meaning to extraclass life than we found in some of the four-year residential colleges. By productive innovation, a perplexing problem had been brought nearer to solution.

THE USE AND ABUSE OF RULES

In terms of student responsibility, we found that rules and regulations on a campus can be both used and abused. We asked ourselves the question, "Does the machinery set up to administer rules and regulations build character as it operates?" The answer, we concluded, depends initially on the attitude of those who establish as well as those who enforce the rules. If there were reasons—sound reasons—behind the rules, we found that students were quick to understand both the reasons and the rules and to cooperate. But it is important for the institution to go out of its way—sometimes far out of its way—to make known the underlying postulates. Misunderstanding wells up quickly, often from apparently trivial causes. One student told us, for instance, "I was put on probation for letting my girl in the side door of the student center during a dance. I was only trying to be a gentleman because she had a light coat on, it was raining, and the line at the front door was very long. You'd think I was a criminal."

The students with whom we talked appeared to resent particularly this lack of faith in them. One commented, "They may educate us, but as far as making us responsible, I'm afraid they lose. With these ridiculous regulations and the corps of police around here, no student is going to be genuinely responsible. Instead, he's tempted to beat the system when he can." And a student wrote to his campus newspaper, "College provides an opportunity to leave home and mother. It should allow a youngster to grow up and learn to run his own life. He will not learn this if a group of . . . busybodies circumscribe his every act more stringently than ever his parents did."

The instances of student understanding and cooperation were far more frequent than infrequent. We found again that students respond when they are told they are adults and are treated as adults. This applies to the majority. The minority, however, is sometimes mistaken for the majority. A senior complained, "Whenever a small group makes trouble, all of us are blamed. When somebody blows a bugle at 2 A.M., some of the faculty get the idea we're all on a toot. I wish a few of these people would remember that they made a little noise when they were young. Furthermore, not all of us are participating in making the noise every minute."

The Potential Benefits

From conversations with students and faculty members as well as observations of the campus scene, it was not difficult to identify the potentially positive results of student assumption of responsibility in extraclass life. Repeatedly students mentioned particular experiences which, they asserted, gave them a better perspective of themselves and of others. Potentially, each campus offers a wide variety of experiences, intellectual and emotional. We did not find, for instance, a single college where at least a sizable number of students were not engaged in some kind of activity beyond the classroom. So long as the college makes possible the time and encourages in this way the inclination to organize and maintain activities, it should also be conscious of the possible values to be derived from them.

On some campuses we found the activities were the most genuine and rigorous test of the student. In qualifying, he was not expected to pass examinations or to receive grades. Either he did the work and was welcomed, or he did not do it and was omitted. It was as simple as that. Furthermore, the lessons to be derived were obvious and the experiences both genuine and rewarding.

PERCEPTION OF SELF AND OTHERS

Learning to work directly with people and gaining understanding of others as well as oneself are benefits derived from properly organized group activity, and we found all kinds of activity on almost every campus. The student mind is amazingly inventive: no matter when or where an interest is shown, usually a committee is appointed, a group organized, a constitution written, and meetings held. As in much of American life, some of this is without apparent value. Students testify, however, to increased understanding of other students more through activity groups than through the usual classroom contact. One commented, "Some students have the narrow attitude that they are here only to study. Once they have a college degree, they can do anything. But as they associate with more and more different people, they begin to open up a bit. Pretty soon they discover they can study and grow more human, both at the same time."

Some of the multiphased campus activities are specifically directed toward improved understanding. An interesting example is the Representative to Russia program at Oberlin College. Annually, each Oberlin student contributes one dollar toward the expense of sending one of his fellow-students to live in Russia for the summer preceding his senior year. The balance of funds necessary for the trip is paid by the student chosen, although this seldom amounts to as much as he might spend on summer study at home. The student returns from Russia to his formal education at Oberlin. During the year following his visit he devotes much of his time to interpreting to his fellow students, in formal and informal sessions, the Russia he has seen. In addition, he makes himself available to groups in the wider community of Oberlin and surrounding cities and towns for speeches describing his experiences. Despite the name of the program, the destination point for the program is not always Russia; last year's student spent the summer in Indonesia. Many with whom we talked at Oberlin attested to their increased understanding of the people of another country gained from one among them with firsthand experience.

Some of the other colleges and universities conduct student exchange programs with other nations, as well as provide for time overseas as part of the student's own curricular pattern. In addition, formal and informal discussions of foreign cultures and international problems are frequent events during the college year. These supplement the curricular offerings. An annual program at the University of Colorado, for instance, is an example of combined faculty and student interest and effort. United Nations Week is sponsored by the students. It is essentially an international festival with displays, foreign student coffee hours and dinners, a model U.N. assembly, an Avenue of Flags from U.N. countries, and a telenews theater showing films on international affairs.

The Conference on World Affairs, held at Colorado during United Nations Week, is sponsored by the department of social sciences. The variety of subjects covered in the panels and lectures is extensive. More than sixty guest speakers are brought to the campus to tell of their particular responsibilities or interests in domestic and foreign affairs. Topics range from foreign trade to current crisis areas to American educational problems. Many faculty members participate in the planning and presentation of the program.

Students at Colorado mentioned the two events frequently in

citing activities which broadened their horizons. An attempt has been made to correlate the curricular and extracurricular efforts. The president of the university has stated that "the activities of the students, the talks, and the discussions are essential parts of our educational program."

We found a number of examples also of attempts through activities to promote student understanding of himself and of his contemporaries. In many cases students gain understanding merely through close association with fellow students from other regions. A sophomore girl reported,

> There are so many different types on this campus—geographic, social, economic—that, just by living with them, we're forced to appreciate different people. I come from the East, for instance. Until I hit college, I thought that people who wore earrings with bobby-sox and loafers were just plain strange. Now I've found out that this is the custom in some parts of the country. And the girls who do it really aren't very different from myself.

More formally organized programs are often coupled with some kind of service endeavor, although many such efforts appear to reach only the relative few who are directly involved. At Stephens College, for instance, the Senior Sisters help make easier the adjustment of new students at the same time that the Sisters find out something about themselves. Each year approximately one hundred and forty girls are carefully selected and systematically trained to act as guides for the entering students. The Senior Sisters (second-year students in the junior college) live in first-year student dormitories. Each assists eight to ten new girls with their academic, social, and personal life.

The Senior Sisters work with each girl individually as well as conduct regularly scheduled meetings of their entire group to assess together the progress made and to uncover special needs. They are available for personal conferences, but they are trained to know when and where to make referrals of problems demanding professional attention. All the Senior Sisters meet periodically to evaluate their work and to discuss methods of improving their services. In outward appearance the program is much like other efforts throughout the country. Its distinction may lie in the depth of training and in the unusual interest of the participating students.

A few institutions have made apparently successful efforts to challenge the individual student to engage in self-analysis and self-development at the same time that he seeks to be of service to others. Freshman Camp at the University of New Hampshire, for instance, is more than the usual three- or four-day program of informal orientation preceding the beginning of the college year. The activity is specifically planned so that the upper-class leaders, who are chosen as counselors, will actually gain from the experience as much as, or more than, the entering student. The heart of the program is the counselor training which encourages each upper-class leader to examine himself before he is placed in the position of helping others.

The camp is completely planned and operated by students who make all the business arrangements, plan the meals, and work out the entire program for the three hundred freshmen who attend. The camp is held at a regular summer camp leased for the occasion. It is located about forty miles from the campus. Approximately sixty counselors are chosen from over two hundred applicants after careful screening and interviewing by the student executive staff. The choice is made early in the second semester, followed by thirteen weeks of training. The counseling staff is required to attend one evening meeting a week, plus numerous subcommittee meetings and an off-campus week-end conference in the spring.

The early part of the training period attempts to focus counselor thinking on themselves. For instance, an evening is devoted to a presentation and discussion of each of the following topics: (1) What makes a good student member of the university community? (2) What are the special responsibilities and privileges of the educated person? (3) What are the special difficulties which students experience in human relations? (4) What difficulties do students experience in relating themselves to meaningful religion?

The counselors carry out the theme of self-analysis in the camp program planned for the freshmen. The camp which we attended devoted an entire morning or afternoon session to each of these questions: What is this university? What's expected of you? What are you going to do about it? Who is this *you?* The latter topic included consideration of past attitudes, ideas, and opinions; the influence of parents, school, friends, and church; what the new student wants from the future and its relationship to the present; and his reasons for coming to college.

The camp appears to be a successful example of an attempt by students, with some faculty guidance in addition, to look more deeply into reasons for attending college, what responsibilities are involved, and what expectations. Many counselors as well as many freshmen reported to us that the experience serves them well in helping to give better background to the decisions facing them.

Other colleges and universities recognize, too, the influence of this type of student orientation by students. Cornell University was one of the earliest freshman camp advocates. It has now suspended its camps in an experiment designed to bring the same kind of student-to-student informal orientation to a campus program involving all entering students. The University of Colorado, a relative newcomer to the camp field, sponsors a freshman camp several weeks after the opening of the college year and after the freshmen have had firsthand experience with the pressures and problems of college life.

Many other campus activities—including charity fund drives, work in local hospitals and orphanages, and deputation teams to rural churches—are designed to lead students to a greater understanding of others at the same time that they learn to work effectively with their fellow students.

DECISIONS AND STANDS AFFECTING A WIDER CIRCLE

An especially important emphasis for young people, inclined to remain in a rut of self-pity and self-indulgence, is the opportunity to make decisions and to take stands which affect a wider circle than the self. Much is said of the special responsibility of college-educated men and women for selfless community service. Our observations lead us to believe, however, that the campus emphasis leans too far in the direction of honoring leadership rather than service. It is particularly troublesome when the college itself throws its weight behind prestige enhancement. One student lamented to us that "in high school they told me I was a leader. When I got to college I was informed that I was now the cream of the crop. I'm getting mighty sick of being on top."

We find that, in order to be meaningful, special attention must be given to the obligations as well as the privileges of leaders. A number of colleges attempt to emphasize service over prestige leadership through annual conferences for the students selected to head major campus organizations. The Universities of Louisville, Arizona, Wisconsin, Colorado, and New Hampshire, for example, bring together faculty members, administrative officers, and students for week-end discussions. The site often is one removed from the busyness of campus life. An unusually successful conference on one campus last year was based on the role-playing technique. As each student or faculty member registered for the conference, he was given a role to play during the week-end discussions. The participant was presented with a description of the type of person he should pretend to be—including the background, interests, and prejudices of the imaginary figure. Those who took part reported to us that, as a result of being someone else for a while, they received unusual insight into how other people viewed their own efforts and campus problems as well.

At the same university a senior honorary society, traditionally a prestige mutual-admiration organization for senior men, took on a new function when it stepped into a troublesome campus situation by sponsoring a particularly controversial speaker and then obtaining a second speaker to present the other side of the argument. The senior men, subject to much pressure and some abuse from a local newspaper, discovered for the first time what it meant to take a stand and to make a decision unpopular with an especially vocal minority. One member of the organization commented to us, "I learned more getting into that situation than I did in many of the courses I've taken during my four years."

Students who thus learn to make decisions may also learn the accompanying lesson of how best to carry out the decision. A sophomore who had worked under one senior gave her the highest compliment when she stated, "That's a girl who can give an order in such a way as to make you want to do it."

On most campuses which we visited students participate also to some degree in the determination and continuing evaluation of educational policy matters. We found an Oberlin committee to be particularly active in this area. Composed jointly of students and faculty members, the students met weekly, with faculty members joining them every other week. Discussions and recommendations covered any concern of students, new and old. On several campuses, students expressed to us genuine unhappiness over the small voice they were given in suggesting what and how they shall be taught. The president of a student council observed, "Our council will never really be satisfied until we can have the opportunity to suggest changes in the curriculum. We certainly don't think we ought to have the final say, but after all, we're the ones who are undergoing this experience. Maybe our opinions once in a while might reveal something."

The student is a reflection of society; of this there are many evidences. We observed, for instance, that the traditional man of character was not always the campus hero. One student took the pessimistic view that "students prefer to hide their convictions under a blanket of superficiality because of the social pressure of the crowd." We attempted to analyze the qualities of the student leaders who were the most highly respected by their fellow students and by the faculty. In almost all cases, incidentally, faculty members and students identified the same leaders. We found that effective leaders appear to have at least two qualities in common: they approach tasks with humility in the recognition that their roles are not greater than they actually are, but they also have self-confidence enabling them to move effectively among their fellow students without seeking the comfort of conformity.

We discovered that the most highly respected student leader generally is not aware that he is setting an example of substantial influence on his fellow students. He is inclined to forget the freshman hero worship in which he, too, engaged several years before. We found this attitude in the extreme at Annapolis where upper-class leaders make a strong impression on the plebes. The impression is not, however, totally without its critical side. As one plebe remarked, "Some upperclassmen give us demerits for a spot or something when they themselves have dirty shoes. Fortunately there isn't too much of this or the plebes would develop the attitude that, once they, too, have reached the upper-class position, they won't have to measure up. This is bad. Then they're not ready for the privileges which accompany that spot."

Though many students do not talk easily about their heroes, some talked to us openly and freely. One student, for instance, mentioned the effect upon him as a freshman of a senior who had been his dormitory counselor. The counselor had written to him during the summer before the student entered college. He had helped him when he first arrived on campus. The student concluded, "This impressed me so much that I've spent the last two years as a counselor myself, trying to help the next ones coming along."

While perhaps it is well that the student leader is not completely aware of his potency as an example, it does not mean that he should not be encouraged in his assumption of responsibilities. We found especially that he needs encouragement from faculty members and administrative officers. His willingness to take a stand, both as a person and in terms of decisions, deserves the support of the adult members of the community. We conclude that the college should look to itself if its student leaders perform with timidity and without apparent conviction. Perhaps the college is guilty of supporting such an approach. Certainly every campus needs to stand behind the students who honestly and conscientiously attempt to serve. For every man or woman of this kind, there may be several others, depending on the campus, who represent an attitude and a point of view which the college would not want to endorse.

REAPPRAISAL OF THE VALUE OF ONE'S WORK

Again, properly organized, student activities can serve the useful purpose of stimulating the student to reappraise both himself and the value of his efforts. To us the chief obstacle preventing this appears to be the strong force for continuity on most campuses, regardless of what is being continued. We found everywhere a need for constant re-evaluation of the value of activities, lest, in the commonly repeated phrase, activity becomes confused with achievement. As long as there exists the dichotomy between academic effort and extracurricular busy work, no controlling purpose will force the re-examination. A dean pointed out that "the educational goals of an individual should be the framework for his extracurricular activities. They should be a fulfillment of need rather than quantity." But too often we found that either the system, the custom, or the tradition was the controlling factor in whether or not students supported particular events or organizations. There appeared to be much deadwood in extra-class life deserving sometimes wholesale pruning. The question *why?* is a neglected interrogation on some campuses.

Another force which prevents or discourages reappraisal appeared to be the dependence of administrative officers and faculty members on students for time-consuming trivia. The potentiality of honorary organizations, for instance, appeared to be dissipated often by the expectation that members should be available at any time to act as hosts or ushers, to pour tea, and to perform a number of other ancillary functions.

We found that a particularly insidious and potentially damaging problem had arisen on a number of campuses because of the combined pressure of student financial need and student apathy. The growth of the practice of paying "salaries" to student officers and managers was reported in many colleges and universities. Faculty advisers mentioned that, as a result, some students were unwilling to take on posts requiring the assumption of responsibility unless they were paid to do so. Again this may be caused by insufficient backing and recognition of the student leader. Whatever the cause, however, the future willingness of some college graduates to be voluntary community leaders appears to us to be endangered.

There is reason to hope that the practice of intelligent, thoroughly honest, and careful reappraisal may be an experience of benefit to the individual student as well as to the activity. Intelligent self-analysis as well as the acquisition of knowledge should result from the collegiate experience.

RECOGNITION OF THE NEED FOR BALANCED LIVING

Wherever we traveled, we found the sentiment that the student, like the faculty member, cannot be expected to work at his job all twenty-four hours of every day. Campus life, therefore, should include a place for healthy, nonacademic recreational activity for which the student assumes responsibility commensurate with effective operation. Competitive athletics are an important part of the balanced life. They offer training and practice in the effective use of leisure time as well as lessons in sportsmanship.

The athletic program at the United States Naval Academy, for example, was mentioned repeatedly by midshipmen as an important supplementary experience. Faculty members asserted that the Academy athletic program illustrates an honest concern for the student as an individual. Sports are viewed as an integral part of the education of each midshipman. Each semester all are required to participate in some form of athletic activity, of which swimming and boxing are compulsory. The main objective of the program was described as an attempt to build confidence, endurance, and agility. Each individual is encouraged to reach his maximum strength and to develop qualities of moral and physical courage, group loyalty, fair play, leadership ability, and quick thinking under pressure. Carry-over sports are particularly emphasized in order that physical fitness may be maintained in later years. The program utilizes what the coaches called the "sympathetic method of teaching." In addition, certain rules apply to all sports, such as the prohibition of swearing and boisterous yelling.

On many campuses the programs of the student unions appeared to give the student an opportunity to deepen nonacademic interests as well as to supplement the academic. A recent study at the University of Wisconsin Student Union indicated that the student who was active in the union carried on his interests by becoming active in community life following graduation. Student activity advisers told us, however, that they can never be certain to what extent the experience of the student actually makes a difference and to what extent the active student would become involved later in life, even if he had not been stimulated by the campus experience. One activity adviser concluded, "We have to be careful that we don't concentrate our efforts only on those who are immediately interested and responsive. They may be the ones who least need the experience."

THE PRODUCTIVE USE OF ENERGIES

The emphasis on student responsibility is both a positive contribution to education and a device to prevent accidents. As John

Sloan Dickey wrote in *The Atlantic* several years ago, "The American male at the peak of his physical powers and appetites, driving a hundred and sixty big white horses across the scenes of an increasingly open society, with week-end money in his pocket and with little prior exposure to trouble and tragedy, personifies an 'accident going out to happen.' "[2] The productive use of energies is, therefore, of great importance for the student. If it can be coupled with lessons in responsibility, it helps to fulfill some of the aims of educating the student for the quality of life he must lead to carry out his promise of significant service.

[2] Dickey, "Conscience and the Undergraduate," in *The Atlantic,* April 1955, p. 31.

6. The Opportunity for Religious Understanding and Practice

> Some people can really get obsessed with seeking perfection in the smaller virtues and lose sight of the bigger ones. Actually, I think a sincere and active love of man and God will, of necessity, lead one to practice all these virtues—you know, the ones like kindness and charity—while still holding the big view in sight.

> Let's get down to the meat of it. I'm interested—deeply interested—in what religion has to offer. I'd like the chance to explore it and maybe to attempt to practice it. But every time I get anywhere near religion, I'm driven away by the pomposity and hypocrisy of some of the believers. Boy, I don't want to be like that. I'd rather stick to my lost old self.

THESE VIGNETTES from conversations reflected the desire and the reaction we frequently found among students. The words were first those of a senior woman and then of a sophomore man with whom we talked. These students mirrored many of their counterparts in wanting to know what religion is all about, in approaching some understanding of it, but also in rejecting sometimes the opportunity because of their concepts of what is involved. We include the opportunity for religious understanding and practice among the elements leading to excellence in character because of the interest and concern on the part of so many whom we met and because we believe the college cannot escape an obligation to deal positively with religion. Many expressed the hope that religion possibly could offer the summing up—the unified approach—in contrast to the fragmentation of values promoted by other influences.

At the same time that we observed this hope, we observed also the profound effect of secularization in American education.

With the exception of some students in the strongly church-centered institutions, as well as a lesser number elsewhere, religion to many college students appears to have little direct relationship to higher learning. And even the church-centered institution must struggle mightily against external pressures on the student. From our interviews and what we listened to in long bull sessions, we conclude that the practical-minded student, living in a pragmatic world, views religion in the main as a mysterious abstraction—something vaguely attractive but not well understood.

Many of the students were deeply introspective. When they considered their lives ahead, they wanted, sometimes with great eagerness, a frame of reference for their lives, but it was not necessarily a religious frame. The introspection was a means to self-identification, not wholly a device for the integration of a philosophy of life. One student told us, for instance, "I live now and in the immediate future because that's all I can see." And another one commented, "We're the ones who are supposed to save the world, but darn if we can find any way to get started. Maybe that accounts for the feeling of futility and for the longing for a rationale among so many of us."

Among the twenty institutions we visited, the religious motivations and interest of both the colleges and students represented a wide range. There were those on some campuses who felt that religion is purely a personal thing and has little to do with the academic experience. Others stated that the college cannot but influence the student in some way and that it must, therefore, take into account the individual's relationship to a higher totality. And, to an even further degree, one young lady reported, "In this college they don't try to pull the rug out from under our religious beliefs, but to make it thicker and firmer. In other words, instead of breaking down and scattering to the wind our religious convictions, they ask us to examine them. They also provide many facilities and opportunities for our beliefs to be strengthened and vitalized."

Some colleges, of course, were founded and continue to function in the spirit of a particular faith. Others seek a religious context which is not denominational. Still others, particularly the publicly supported institutions, contend that it is not their business to promote one faith but only to make available the opportunity for the practice of all faiths in accordance with the interest and desire of each person.

The Student Views Religion

In contrast to the contentions of some people, we found no religious revival on the campuses we visited. There was an honest interest in what religion has to offer; on some campuses, administrative officers and chaplains reported an increase in the number attending chapel and church services; but nowhere did we come across the kind of fervent concern and activity on the basis of which one might affirm that a revival was taking place. On the other hand, contrary to some accusations, we did not find the college student to be antireligious. We would term it, rather, in many cases a suspension of consideration and a questioning of the traditional approaches to religious belief. Students of all faiths, as well as those with no fixed beliefs, told us again and again that they were uninspired by the usual pattern of religious activity. One student commented, "I don't care too much for religion as such but I do enjoy singing in the choir. And I find I'm getting to like church more, especially when I see good, healthy men there and not just old ladies, as in my church at home."

Not infrequently we came upon the student who was exploring on his own. On the one hand, he reacted against those with fixed beliefs, and, on the other hand, he conveyed to us a yearning for something to which he might be able to give his loyalty. As one stated, "I guess religion is important for a good many people. It's a chain in their nose which guides them, and keeps them from running away. I don't have any formal religion, but I'm developing one of my own. I'm not an atheist, though." And a Roman Catholic student observed, "I go to Mass but I don't get anything out of it. This bothers me, so I've decided to start way back and take a look at everything again. Before long I'll probably ask the priest for help, but right now this has to be me on my own."

We are led to believe that the student response to religion is conditioned heavily by the current strongly relativistic social thought. Many students react against absolutism in any form, and, to them, religion is purely and simply absolutism. In some cases their rejection of it is emotional as well as intellectual. We asked students, for instance, "What convictions do you have about which you're absolutely certain?" In response, many were at a loss for anything to say. The most common answer—and yet the one offered by less than a third of those questioned—was a belief in the existence of God. A few mentioned faith in the dignity of man or in individualism of some form. But, over-all, this question left most students bewildered. Obviously they had not given much thought to their basic notions about life. Once challenged in this way, however, a number of them became extremely interested in their inability to answer. It was not uncommon for them to seek us out later for further discussion or to raise the topic in a subsequent bull session.

We found that most students associate morality with their inability to comprehend absolutism. For example, many expressed an inability to understand and make significant in their lives what they termed the "vestiges" of a God-centered system of self-discipline to which their grandparents had subscribed (and their parents less so). They contended that the system had been diluted by generations of growing questioning. To them it involved more compromise and hypocrisy than they wished to embrace. On exploring this further, we noted their inclination to accept group standards as criteria rather than individually held values which most religions emphasize. Nevertheless, they regarded morals as a completely personal matter. A sizable number of students appeared to us to be less concerned about their moral reputation than about their success in "life"—meaning, to them, the job and the family. They seemed to feel that there is no connection between success and morality.

This latter reaction led us to explore further the bases on which students make moral decisions while they are in college. What we report here is certainly not true of all with whom we talked, but we believe it represents a fair majority. The criterion most frequently voiced was whether or not one would get caught doing what he was not supposed to do. "I'll take my chances" was a phrase repeated over and over. It applied, for instance, to cheating, sexual promiscuity, and drinking where drinking is frowned upon. Because of social concepts of morals, students were apt to accept dishonesty, sexual activity, drinking, swearing, and so on, as the great moral issues with which they had to deal. They stated that they could see no reason why they should not indulge except that, once detected, it might prove embarrassing or place a block in their progress toward a successful career. Many students did add that what they might do today had no particular relation to what they *would* do tomorrow. There is apparently, then, a double standard—take your chances today but expect that you'll play it safe in the future.

Obviously religion, properly presented and encouraged on a campus, can challenge directly the moral assumptions of many students. It has succeeded in some cases which we encountered. For example, a senior spoke of the "town girl" he was dating. He said, "I've had plenty of opportunity to do some damaging things with her, but my religion always stopped me." A sophomore girl attested to the effect of a chaplain in deepening her convictions. She stated, however, that she still had hesitancy in prescribing for others and certainly in judging others. Her comment: "I won't use a falsified identification card and I won't loan somebody else mine to use falsely, but I'm not about to turn in another girl who does."

It is not surprising to us that the student, increasingly aware of personal and world tensions, and lacking a perspective not unlike his adult counterparts, seeks some foundation for his expanding horizons. The kind of religion he seeks, however, is not always what he regards as the traditional Puritan ethic with its moral inflexibility. This fails the rational test to which he claims to put all ideas of life. If he is expected to be inflexible morally, he must know the reason why.

There is an obvious confusion in the minds of many students between religion and humanitarianism. Religion sometimes is reduced to mere natural philanthropy. The emphasis, however, on helping others which is found in all religions does have an appeal to the student. As a junior mentioned, "I get my biggest kick out of doing things for other people." The element of service appeals to the idealism of some students. We noted on one campus that a student group had capitalized on this attraction. An organization of veterans had been attempting to build up the prestige of their group. They concluded that the best way to gain recognition on their particular campus was to become service-oriented. Their program henceforth consisted of raising funds for the campus chest and other charity drives through the sponsorship of a variety of campus activities.

Intellectualizing Religion

We observed that today's student on the campuses we visited was not particularly glib, nor was he attracted by, and ready to repeat, the catch phrases which have characterized some of his predecessors. To us, he appeared interested in touching fire but afraid of being burned. Instead of jumping at ideas, he held them at a safe distance. In particular, his reaction to religion illustrated his desire to intellectualize what may have been accepted more quickly in previous generations. Perhaps this accounts for the lack of strong and sincere interest on many campuses in organized religious clubs and groups. A majority of students, for instance, felt that religion should be open to the same kind of scrutiny applied to other fields. In addressing a student group, a chaplain on one campus reflected the commonly held student position. He stated, "It is time that the religious communities recognize that their only salvation lies within their willingness to open their dogmatic chambers to the questing spirit of man—to the community set aside in our society for the free pursuit of knowledge."

Not all that we have reported thus far is intended to contradict the kind of genuine interest in religion which we found everywhere. We observed that students respond to the religious stimulus when properly aroused and directed, but it must be in keeping with all else that is happening to them on a campus. As we have stated previously, students are engaged in an honest search for meaning. There may be few of the usual "conversions" in college, but religion does have an extremely important role to play in helping students regroup and restate their growing convictions. In the fall of 1954, for example, the Harvard University Student Council organized a committee to write a report on religion in the college. Eight students of various religious views, after careful study and research, prepared a thirty-nine-page document on the place of religious thought in Harvard and the influence of the college on religious faith.[1] It is a splendid example of serious student consideration of basic problems. The report states, "Students think about the most profound questions of their lives in religious symbols. Beyond doubt their interest in religious issues is keen. To avoid discussing these things is to neglect a responsibility and an opportunity."

Students in every college we visited indicated an interest in finding more realistic and informative opportunities to confront religion. One faculty member at a state university noted the increasing concern among students "for the opportunity to study

[1] *Religion at Harvard* (Cambridge, Mass.: Harvard Student Council, 1956).

religion with the same academic respectability as they might study English literature." He predicted mounting pressure for honest religious instruction, devoid of proselytizing. A student newspaper on another campus affirmed that religious instruction must be "critical, expository, never polemical or dogmatic [and] never designed to convert the student."

We found students continually suspicious of the way religion might be taught. Many felt, often without apparent foundation, that the teaching would lapse into preaching. One faculty member went out of her way to emphasize to her students that she would not indulge in what she called "pious piffle" in teaching. Our observations lead us to believe that the manner in which religion is approached in the curriculum does reflect to some degree the entire religious tone of the college.

Most students felt strongly that religion has a place in the curriculum because, as the Harvard student report noted, it "deals directly with questions of faith and ultimate meaning" in which the student is deeply interested. The Harvard report concluded, "the fact that religion treats life whole, and proposes conceptions of ultimate worth which have vitalized the thinking and lives of many, suggest it as an effective avenue for approaching ultimate questions."

Many students hope religion can be rationally approached before it is emotionally embraced—a sentiment with which many of their chaplains appear to agree. A professor of philosophy spoke of it in this way:

A philosophy of life is never what is so commonly called an opinion or a set of opinions. At least that isn't what a respectable philosophy of life is. It may incidentally be that which I happen to believe, but that isn't the way I define it or describe it. It isn't an opinion, and it isn't a set of opinions. It has to be understood as a *position*. This is something which we can confirm by evidence or which invites refutation —something which can be argued and defended. And also something which can be continuously expanded and yet has in it a continuity that makes it a position of which we are aware.

Vitality and Relevancy

When we attempted to pin down what appeals to the student, we discovered immediately that vitality and relevancy are essential if religion is to elicit continuing student interest and participation. In this area above all others, tradition alone is not enough. For example, most of the campuses we visited sponsor, in some form, required or voluntary chapel services. But the success of these services, no matter what the form, is dependent on the relevancy of the service, the sermons, and the personality of the preachers. A student in one college reflected what a number of others also said when he commented, "Before I go to chapel, I look to see who's preaching. We get some good speakers here and some poor ones. I prefer, naturally, to hear only the good. It's the only way I get anything out of going to church."

Similarly, it appears that Roman Catholic students seek a more understanding participation in liturgical worship rather than to be merely passive spectators at liturgical rites.

At Stephens College an attempt is made to keep the Protestant vesper service relevant at all times. An active student-faculty committee informally polls the campus to determine pertinent problems, pressures, or questions. The results are brought to the attention of the dean of religious life, one of the five top administrative officers of the college. He discusses with the committee the kind of service to be offered each week. After each service, the committee surveys attitudes and reactions to determine if the need has been met. Jointly, students and faculty attempt to make vespers an integral part of the educational process.

Roman Catholic colleges make an attempt to permeate the entire collegiate experience with a spirit of religious dedication. The effort is aided, of course, by a student body which, by virtue of its choice of the college, is willing to accept greater religious emphasis, but the college seeks much more than the minimum. It makes readily available a number of opportunities. The University of Notre Dame, for example, has developed a substantial religious program in its highly conscious attempt to graduate men of sound character. The university acts on the basis of its belief that character is the habit of principled action and that the ideal graduate of a Catholic college is one who thinks, judges, and acts consistently in accordance with right reason illumined by the supernatural light of the example and teaching of Christ.

Every Catholic student at Notre Dame is required to take courses in religion so that he may achieve a deeper understanding of the Catholic faith and the nature of Christian living. Other students may elect to take these courses. All are required to enroll in a prescribed number of courses in philosophy. As one faculty member described it, "We make a conscious attempt to lead the student to a set of reasoned principles on which to base morality and to help him develop facility in the application of these principles to actual life."

The institution also offers the opportunity wherever possible for individual guidance to supplement the classroom instruction. A chaplain and his assistants are available at all times for counsel, together with the resident priests who administer each dormitory. Priests who are members of the faculty live on each floor of the Notre Dame dormitories. The prefects, as they are called, supervise the discipline of the hall as well as guide and counsel the students under their charge. The university attempts to select men who, through example and association, will help the students. In order to make religious worship readily available and to capture spontaneity of feeling, each dormitory has a chapel in which students may attend the daily morning Mass. Students are strongly encouraged to attend at least three times a week.

An organization on the campus of Notre Dame, as well as at other Roman Catholic colleges, which dedicates itself in a special way to character formation is the Sodality of Our Lady. The top students on the campus are chosen to undergo a period of probation usually involving weekly study, instruction, and discussion of the rules of the society, including their significance and relevance to high standards of Christian living. The emphasis is on personal excellence in life and service to others. The candidate for admission ordinarily studies this way of life for six months or a year under the guidance of present members. He attempts to live up to the obligations thus imposed. If he wishes, he may then associate himself with the sodality as a member. If he is adjudged worthy of membership, he is received into the association and professes his dedication to its ideals. The students with whom we talked mentioned frequently the effect of sodality membership on the entire campus.

Roman Catholic students at Catholic colleges are expected also to participate in retreats, a period of reflective prayer varying in length from one or two days to a week or more. The student during the retreat is encouraged, under the guidance of an experienced spiritual director, to measure his habits and actions by the standard of the highest spiritual and moral principles as enunciated by the Church. The retreats usually occur in the first semester in order that greater meaning and direction may be given to the coming year.

On many campuses special emphasis is given religion in the form of Religious Emphasis, or Religious Focus, or Religion-in-Life Weeks, a period of seven days of lectures, discussions, and sometimes exhibits and plays. The programs from campus to campus vary greatly in form and potency. Their very continuance does indicate a continuing interest on the part of the student. Some students and more faculty members voiced criticism of what they called "the one-shot kicker for religion," with the implication that if religion is to have vitality, it must be emphasized every day rather than one week each year.

The Service Approach

We found that a surprising number of students who purposefully and successfully resist approaches to the usual kind of religious activities do participate actively in the so-called service programs found on almost every campus. In many colleges the

YMCA and YWCA provide the administrative organization. Oberlin College, for example, has an extensive Y program in which a large number of students participate. Radcliffe College, which tends to de-emphasize participation in denominational groups, cooperates with Harvard in the extensive Phillips Brooks House program. Activities include a wide range of volunteer work on behalf of less fortunate people in the wider community. The Burrall program at Stephens College, primarily a service organization, involves over half the student population each year in volunteer work. The larger campuses are served by denominational groups of a wide variety.

It was obvious to us that students are willing to give of themselves and their time to significant causes. Many with whom we talked professed impatience with the kind of religious activity which speaks of piety and self-righteousness without adequate recognition that it is often in losing one's self that a new life emerges. It was surprising, however, to find that the effect of participation in religious activity groups did not appear to spread beyond those directly involved. Where it does permeate, the quality of the religious community is obviously an important factor. We observed several denominational groups, for instance, on four campuses which were highly regarded and apparently influential. The sample was too small to make a valid generalization but we did find that each of these groups had made a special effort to enlist the interest and participation of the strongest student leaders, thereby initially borrowing prestige for the group. On other campuses, it appeared that students remained away from religious groups because "the kids are apt to ridicule you. They really don't mean it, but it's fashionable to a cynic—and religion is a prime target for the cynic."

Interfaith Interest and Effort

We encountered many students who were especially interested in interfaith relations. Though they are often ignorant of the bases of their own faiths, the beliefs of others hold a certain fascination for college students. Some, for instance, would rather know about Confucianism than about why they are Baptists. On a few campuses successful cooperative programs involving the major faiths have been organized, partly to coordinate denominational efforts and partly through the interests of the students who have difficulty understanding why denominational groups with many of the same aims have so much trouble working together. As an editorial in a campus newspaper stated, "We can no longer afford the luxury of religions that raise barriers between men. With death and destruction the penalty for lack of understanding, religion must take a new tack and seek to spread quieting oil on the troubled waters of tension and hatred."

We conclude that in almost all instances the success of the interfaith effort hinges on the willingness of the clerical participants to work together with all that cooperative effort implies. In some instances, for example, failure has been due to some of the Protestant chaplains who expect all interfaith efforts to be essentially Protestant. This is especially true of worship services in which the Roman Catholic priest and the rabbi have been criticized for not participating. In other instances, the Roman Catholic representative gave only token support or none at all to the interfaith program. In still other cases, the various clergy were unable to work in unison largely, apparently, because of personality conflicts. Any interfaith effort, we find, must recognize first the common points of view and then recognize honestly and openly the differing as well as noncompatible viewpoints. We have observed that students everywhere find little difficulty in working constructively with men and women of other faiths; they do have difficulty, however, understanding the incompatibility of the adult leadership.

One of the most highly organized and most interesting programs to be found on a non-church-related campus is the Cornell United Religious Work at Cornell University. CURW, as it is commonly called, is an interfaith, campus-centered effort which aims "to promote and strengthen the religious, intellectual, social, and moral life of the students." The program is organized around the common assumptions of the great religious faiths. It attempts to offer students greater freedom and adaptability within the various shades of religious interest. As a result, we found that it does attract many students who do not respond to the organized church programs of a single denomination. CURW strives also to offer a means for students and faculty members to work together in maintaining high standards of religious influence in campus life. In addition to this strong, central interfaith emphasis, CURW is composed of a number of constituent religious groups which function as the primary campus units for work with students in their particular denominations.

Organizationally, the program operates under a university board of control with student and faculty representation. Three full-time professional people direct the interfaith work. In addition, most of the twelve participating denominational groups have one or more chaplains or advisers. Each member group and its adviser is expected to devote some time to the cooperative effort which includes such activities as freshman orientation, study groups, a One World Club, foreign student activities, an annual and apparently highly successful Campus Conference on Religion, and deputations to high schools. The majority of activities take place within Annabel Taylor Hall, a handsome and functional home for CURW located near the center of the Cornell campus.

The Importance of Leadership

Wherever the campus and whatever its religious orientation, we found that the quality of the adult leader was a strongly determining factor in the success or failure of the religious emphasis. We observed that his personality, wisdom, ability to work with students, and his reputation (which soon became known to all) determined often the depth of the religious impact. Frequently students asserted that personal contact was among the strongest, if not actually the strongest, influence in the shaping of their religious faith. Often where we found a number of students able to discuss religion intelligently and not embarrassed to profess a belief, we found also a minister, priest, rabbi, or professional worker who accounted in part for their interest. One student told us, for instance, "We had a good priest here two years ago. He was very friendly and really seemed to understand our problems. The priest we have now is not very understanding; he doesn't give us any credit for what we may know. His sermons are below our mentality. He talks as though fear were the only motivation for faith."

For this reason, among many, it is evident to us that the various denominations have a strategically important responsibility in placing the right person in the position of working with students. Particularly in the non-church-centered college, the church is likely to leave the so-called future leader of society in the hands of underpaid, poorly supported, and sometimes inadequately trained personnel. Immediately these people are rejected by the campus community for their inability to fit into the academic environment. An editorial in one student paper reflected the feeling of others with whom we talked on a variety of campuses. It commented:

It is the religious leaders who have rejected the campus by their unwillingness to abide by the standards of a community of scholars. It is not the other way around: the campus has not rejected religion; rather, the religious leaders have literally turned their backs on the educative experience. As long as the religious groups conceive of themselves as street venders of unwavering ideas, they will remain on the outside of this community of scholars, who are charged with an unswerving quest of knowledge and an acceptance of the uncertain conclusions to which their quest may lead them.

Though they should hold to their convictions, denominational representatives should also take into account the workings of the community of which they are a part; otherwise, they may negate their opportunities.

The right kind of adult leader, as we observed him, fashioned with his students the effective approach. He did not depend on methods of recruiting which would lower the dignity of religion in the minds of the students. Above all, the student wants a dignified and intelligent approach to religion. On one campus, for instance, students pointed with disgust and dismay to the denominational folder which had been sent to their parents in a fund-raising effort. On it appeared a picture of a dance with the caption, "Students enjoy wholesome fellowship together, with Jesus Christ as chaperone."

Beyond the organized religious groups, we found some signs of a growing movement among the students themselves to encounter religion. As an example, a junior girl and her roommate in one dormitory had purchased together a number of religious books. They found that the books interested the other girls who came to their room, so they set up an informal lending library. The junior estimated that so far probably twenty-five or thirty girls had read one book and then another and another. She commented, "I'm amazed at the interest they show in reading about religion. They like a clear-cut, well-organized, and persuasive treatment. I've noticed, too, that titles with the word 'meaning' immediately attract them."

Occasionally we encountered instances in which students and faculty members together explored religious questions outside of the formal curriculum. The attitude of faculty members toward religion frequently influenced the thinking of the student. A few campuses sponsored conferences, on and off campus, for common discussion of religious problems facing both faculty members and students. One psychology professor told us that, in his view, religion offers a common level of interest and challenge. Other faculty members, however, complained of the religious illiteracy of the student. One was especially vehement on the subject when he stated, "Students today have incredibly poor religious orientation before coming to college. It makes communication extremely difficult." We might agree with his conclusion but not with his comparison. Either the professor was a product of a strong church family or the victim of a poor memory.

The Campus Religious Climate

Initially, the student choice of a church-centered college makes easier the task of creating a religious climate on the campus of that college. The nonsectarian college is, however, a composite of many faiths and degrees of faith; an even greater interest and direction is required if its religious life is to have vitality. Dartmouth College is presently engaged in setting up a new and interesting approach. The trustees of the college have established the William Jewett Tucker Foundation "for the specific purpose of supporting and furthering in all ways and in all areas the moral and spiritual work of the college."

The foundation takes its aim and scope from the words of Dr. Tucker, the last of the preacher-presidents of Dartmouth. In a chapel service at the turn of the century he stated, "I make no closing plea for any formal religion, but I do plead now as always for the religious spirit. . . . Seek, I pray you, moral distinction. Be not content with the commonplace in ambition or intellectual attainment. Do not expect that you will make any lasting or very strong impression on the world through intellectual power without the use of an equal amount of conscience and heart."

The dean of the Tucker Foundation will have opened for him not only the province of the college chapel but the campus as a whole. He is charged with the encouragement of moral concern and responsibility. In commenting on the newly created position, Dartmouth's President John Sloan Dickey noted, "It is one of both scope and prestige which, while rooted in the religious spirit, could open to its occupant the kind of intimate but wide ranging relationship to the campus that our highly departmentalized colleges so badly need."

On the basis of our study we do not believe that students are antireligious. Though there is no apparent revival in progress, the students we met appeared ready and often eager to explore what religion might bring to them. Certainly it is a frequent topic for discussion. At the same time that they are wrapped in their own tiny world, they look with interest upon the possibility of becoming vital and active evidences of the doctrines they appear to avoid. They will not, however, respond to empty moralizing. They will not commit themselves until they have found what they consider adequate grounds for commitment. Almost every other realm of man's searching and questioning is treated with respect, integrity, and discipline. Many students seek no more than this in appraising man's relationship to God.

This, we believe, places a special responsibility not alone upon the colleges but upon the churches, and, in some instances, the churches obviously have been neglecting college youth. The fact that sometimes religion is not fashionable on a campus seems to us to represent not a barrier but a challenge. It means an extra effort to make sure that the student is offered the possibility of gaining the direction and the confidence, the honest love of God and man, and the greater awareness of the infinite and the universal which sound religious faith may bring to him.

7. *The Effect of Environment*

I can remember opening up the Freshman Handbook to that center spread with the map of the campus. All those buildings with strange new names. I just couldn't believe I'd ever be at home in that place. And then the thousands of faces when I arrived on campus. It was . . . well, just a mass of impressions. I suppose it took me almost a year to make sense of it all. I began to see that, though there were many small units all revolving almost within themselves, the whole thing added up. It is sort of like a clock with lots and lots of tiny pieces inside, but, when they all start moving in unison, the whole business begins to tick and tells time.

SHE WAS a junior; she was majoring in history and hoped some day that she might be teaching it in a college; and she was trying to tell us what had made the deepest impression on her thus far in her own college career. She had found it difficult to single out one course or one person or one experience. "I guess it's the whole thing," she told us. "I feel so sorry for those who don't sense what's going on around this place. They are in the middle of something but never a part of it. They see the wheels revolving but they don't hear the ticking."

In this chapter—the final one of those devoted to the six characteristics of excellence—we will attempt to discuss particular aspects of the whole. An all too common conception of a college education is that it includes only the narrowly defined academic process involving just the teacher and the student. Many college graduates agree, however, that their education took place as much outside the classroom as within its narrow walls, and was as much a result of all that surrounded them as of the formal lecture or seminar. Some refer to this larger, encompassing classroom as "the climate of the campus." We call it the environment.

But, no matter what term is used, we identify it as a factor of paramount significance in the development of character. More than this, we found that particular aspects of the environment have the power either to reinforce or to negate all else that happens. The attitudes, the surroundings, the extra activities, the manners and morals of a campus, for example, can either stimulate or stultify the purely academic endeavor. If learning is to be on a high level, we believe that all else must support it.

In the process of living and learning the student shapes his character for good or for ill. We have already discussed some aspects of environment—for instance, the level of expectancy, the teaching, the curriculum, student responsibility, and the religious life. All these are a part of what surrounds the student. At this point we will deal principally with the nonacademic influences which we have not discussed in full as yet, although we do not mean to imply that environment consists only of these particular influences.

Initially the quality of the environment is established by the level of expectancy. When a high level does *not* permeate the entire campus, however, units of the environment proceed quickly and easily to negate the desired expectancy. The words of Woodrow Wilson put the campus community to an important test:

> My plea then is this, that we now deliberately set ourselves to make a home for the spirit of learning; that we reorganize our colleges on the lines of this simple conception, that a college is not only a body of studies but a mode of association. . . . It must become a community of scholars and pupils—a free community but a very real one, in which democracy may work its reasonable triumphs of accommodation, its vital processes of union.

Our visits to twenty colleges and universities convinced us that the campus is no longer the all-encompassing kind of atmosphere some assume it to be. Two factors made this immediately apparent: the number of students working part time in the larger community to help finance their education, and the mobility of the modern college student. On almost every campus we visited, for instance, the parking of student automobiles was a troublesome administrative problem. Even Oberlin College, long known as a bicycle college where student cars are prohibited, was in the midst of a heated student-faculty debate on a revision of its rules. In many respects the campus has ceased to be a cloistered community in which students reside for months at a time.

We discovered, as one would expect, that the differences in the size, type, and control of colleges presented also wide differences in environment. What applied to the large, heterogeneous campus was not applicable to the small, more closely-knit academic community. The environment of the University of Louisville or of Pasadena City College, for instance, was a far cry from that of Saint Mary's College or of tiny, rural Goddard in the hills of Vermont. The nonresidential institution, especially, must struggle constantly to maintain a productive climate. Its students spend the major portion of their time off campus, away from the influences which affect so profoundly the relatively isolated college in the rural setting. Further than this, the college must take into account the surrounding community. Even Goddard students and faculty members mentioned, for instance, what the people "in town" think of them. And at the University of Notre Dame certain areas of the neighboring city of South Bend had to be considered out of bounds. Though the pattern changes from campus to campus, students still are students. We found marked similarity among the college youth with whom we lived and to whom we talked. Certain conclusions may be drawn in the relationships between environment and character which apply to the majority.

The Setting of Standards

Wherever we traveled we found that the setting of standards was a group process. We encountered relatively few students who professed to maintain (or even hoped to maintain) individually held values sufficiently inviolable to be immune from the sentiment of the group. Where a strong shared conviction did not permeate the campus, the student appeared to fall back upon some familiar group to guide what he thought and did. Or, in some cases, it was a tradition. At an Ivy League institution, the typical student comment went something like this: "Very few students here seem to act or express themselves as they really are. The pressure to be Ivy is really great. Ivy students must drink; Ivy students must not show they are studying. A typical Ivy man doesn't need advice because he can get along fine without restrictions. He's a man. His concern is himself, not others and the outside world." This was the group standard; fortunately, however, it was applied by the individual in less conforming terms.

Again, devoid of the shared conviction, we found that the student protected himself sometimes by this group activity against the influences around him. He did not come to college to have "good" done unto him, and he resisted any semblance of anyone doing "good." We participated in one fraternity group, for instance, which was discussing an administrative move to lift the level of fraternity operations. One student commented, "Why don't they let us alone? I like this fraternity because it's the one place on the campus where I can really be myself." In this setting students appeared to us to come to a reasonable working agreement on what they would or would not accept. Individually, they indicated that they would anticipate being different after college, in accordance with the desires of others, but right now they wanted to be a part of college, which meant to them their immediate surroundings. The plebes at the Naval Academy, for example, were under duress from the midshipmen. They told us that in these conditions, "You learn to need others." Their security lay in the acceptance that all were "suffering" together.

We found evidence, too, that the group tended sometimes to snuff out the informal testing of new ideas. The transmission of

standards and ideas became a rigid operation with no questioning tolerated. As for performance, the institution might
state in a general way its rules and regulations governing conduct, but the only ones rigidly followed in many cases were the
ones rigidly enforced. The size of the particular group which set
the standards, we found, depended in part on the size of the particular college. When the campus was small, homogeneous, and/
or rested upon some particularly strong tradition, standards were
influenced more strongly by the total community. In the larger,
more diversified institution, the students sought out a smaller
group which served both as a focal point for their interests and a
behavior determinant. It was surprising to note that in only a few
isolated cases was the over-all campus governing body, despite
its vigor and respect, especially effective in molding opinions or
setting standards. Furthermore, it did not follow necessarily, that
group standards were always lower than individually held values.
This depended on the purpose and motivation of the group.
More often than not, however, we discovered that the group did
tolerate attitudes and actions unacceptable to the individual on
his own.

We have been speaking here of campuses which were largely residential and in which the higher level of expectancy had not
taken hold. On the nonresidential campus we found an interesting difference. Here student after student pointed to parents and
home life as being influential in their attitudes and thinking.
With this they coupled the influence of the social group with
which they were associated. As one student told us, "We have
one foot on and the other off the campus. I guess, because we
live at home, we haven't yet made a complete break from our
families." On one campus, for instance, strong off-campus social
groups were described as small, self-operating cliques which had
proven to be a negative influence. The groups had been banned
from the campus a few years ago. Students found it difficult to
relate themselves to a campus group (of which there were few),

and some students were actively interested in reinstating campus fraternities to fill the void.

This pattern suggested to us that students adopt their habits of thought and action from that group which happens to be closest to them. They "take on" the attitudes of those with whom they live and with whom they spend their social hours. In the residential college this happens to be the peer group, but in the nonresidential college it can be both the family and the outside gang.

On the basis of what we have seen, we conclude that the student, despite his more apparent shortcomings, is no better and no worse than the average American adult. He is a conformist along with most of his contemporaries. He adapts himself to the group around him. As one noted, "I think it's just conforming to whatever sort of people you are around. It may be a sorority group or a bunch of kids in the dorm. It's whatever friends you happen to have at the moment, or whatever people you happen to be associated with." And another student added, "Let's not think we're alone. The faculty on this campus conform, too. When you analyze it, they set a neat example."

In most colleges which we visited we found that student and faculty conformity was so much the rule that we questioned whether the genuine, sincere individualist could ever be accepted. We were tempted to wonder, for instance, what might happen to a student with ability who refused completely to go along with the group. A faculty member posed this question in an unusual way when he stated, "I don't know how a person with, for instance, the force and conviction of Jesus would get along here. I'm sure he wouldn't last long in a fraternity and probably not in most classes."

There is an important other side to the coin of conformity. We believe that the college need not be satisfied with simply bemoaning the effect of the group. We have seen that it can, if it will, provide an environment in which its level of expectancy becomes the accepted pattern. It can, if it will, take advantage of conformity and create within subsidiary groups the conditions within which educational ideas and ideals may flourish. This becomes, then, Woodrow Wilson's "mode of association . . . a free community but a very real one." Further than this, we discovered latent student interest in breaking the group bonds, but it appeared to be held down by the society around it. For example, an editorial in one campus newspaper commented:

> We are the antiseptic generation. We have grown up protected from the germs of extremisms which had given our elders a case of intellectual gout. For us history is a study only of the past; greatness today is not our necessity. Therefore, we concentrate on "life adjustment" which helps us rid ourselves of the little idiosyncrasies of which greatness is made. [Malcontentism] is as great a sin as adultery and probably more often punished. But somewhere in the back of our minds we know that this protection is but a flimsy wrap. We want to know more, hear more, do more, think more, but our society neither encourages nor rewards those who inquire.

The Contagion of Intimacy

We have already taken the position that the college's best contribution to character is a direct product of the proper, balanced emphasis on learning. To contribute to character, the environment, therefore, must reflect this commitment to learning as the *raison d'etre* of all that happens on the college campus and to the college student. From our study we believe that this can be done without emphasis solely on pure learning as the only end. We believe there exists a pattern which allows the student to study well, which reinforces his learning, and which offers him opportunity also for healthful recreation. Such a pattern helps the student achieve some measure of emotional as well as intellectual maturity.

For a descriptive phrase we turn to Edmund Sinnott's volume *The Biology of the Spirit.* In referring to a factor of strong influence on all living things, Dr. Sinnott speaks of "the contagion of intimacy," meaning what is most intimate to us is apt to be most contagious.[1] An organism adapts itself to its environment; we "soak up" that which surrounds us. We found this obviously to be true of college students. We conclude that one of the most unfortunate mistakes in some colleges is the failure to realize the full potential of the contagion, the failure to come to grips with the student where he is found, and the tendency to leave to tradition, chance, or student device all else but the purely academic.

We discovered, of course, that the right environment, the effective contagion, does not take place automatically. Some assume that one needs only classrooms and dormitories, books, a faculty, and some students. Effective contagion is much more. We believe it is the result of unity in common goals, a communicated tradition to which all phases of campus life make their particular contribution.

In attempting to analyze and identify the components, we found that this contagion appeared to begin with the very physical arrangement of the campus as a whole. The thoughtful planning which goes into the design and placement of buildings, the care with which physical facilities are kept, and the opportunity for expressing love of beauty in the whole as well as its parts are of importance. A college president mentioned this when he told us, "We think the students ought to be surrounded by the kind of campus arrangements which indicate an order, a peace, an appreciation of the richness which can be found in life." As might be expected, many students with whom we talked viewed their physical surroundings as a symbol of their education, the tangible expression of their own aspirations in learning.

On the other side, we noted how inadequate planning on a campus sometimes led to unforeseen and unfortunate results. This is particularly true where it encouraged, rather than helped to reduce, other negative factors in campus living. The distance, for instance, between living units and the main academic build-

[1] Sinnott, *The Biology of the Spirit* (New York: Viking Press, 1955), p. 97 ff.

ings, including the library, often indicated a psychological as well as a physical separation. This was true not only of the large university where space is a problem. We found a relatively small college to be a graphic example of disconnected roots. On the campus of this college, a wide street separated the academic buildings on one side from a row of fraternities on the other. To us and to many of the students the academic program of this institution was strong and compelling. But the fraternities on the opposite side of the road appeared to have little sense of responsibility to or for what happened across the street. As a result, the student was challenged and inspired until he crossed back "home" where he found an entirely different kind of emphasis.

In the physical surroundings, small items as well as the large were indicative also of the campus climate. With some amazement, we found that we could judge a campus fairly well by what was displayed most prominently in the bookstore. If banners and decorated beer mugs were the first items to hit the eye, then we could tell almost always what to expect. If, however, the college had gone out of its way to provide facilities for students to browse among shelves displaying the better books, we were prepared to find a different kind of interest. We discovered, too, that subconsciously students and faculty alike were prone to condition themselves in a dingy environment to a dingy education. The conditions were the symbol of quality, a reaction not uncommon in all American life.

We noted with interest the beginning attempts in some of the larger universities to break down the barriers of size. Several administrative officers talked of decentralization, thus bringing certain advantages of the smaller college to units within the whole. This, they felt, might help to personalize the academic experience. They talked of units which would include living quarters as well as academic buildings according to general fields of study. At the same time they felt that they did not want to lose the great advantages offered in the larger, multipurpose, cosmopolitan university. Whatever the answer, it was obvious to us that both large and small institutions should be more aware of the contribution which the physical surroundings can make to the unity of the campus.

The Spirit of Community

Beyond this tangible substance of buildings and hallways and classrooms and pathways, we found an intangible element which we believe is essential to a spirit of community. Essentially it is effective communication among the various groups on the campus. In too many instances we observed that the communication appeared woefully inadequate; often it was given no special effort and, hence, happened only by chance. Over and over again on some campuses students and faculty members complained that they didn't "know what was going on."

On some campuses we noted that the student newspaper was an important medium of communicating what was happening. There were some instances, however, in which the purposes and horizons of the campus newspaper were too limiting. We found many who felt that the newspaper has a dual role to play in interpreting not just the campus society but national and world events for which the student some day would be assuming an increasing measure of responsibility. As part of our study, we followed closely the news and editorial comment in the newspapers on the campuses we visited (where a regular edition was published). Our general impression was that the student paper allowed itself too often to be concerned with trivia and had too little sense of responsibility for communication. We should add, however, that we were impressed by the increasing amount of space that some of the student newspapers are giving to discussion of the goals of education and curricular matters.

Beyond student effort, keeping people informed adequately begins, we believe, with the attitude of the president. The occasional student assembly or faculty meeting is not enough.

There must be, we conclude, a continuity through a deliberate attempt to make all on a campus feel that each is an important part. The president can also contribute to this just by being available. On one campus, for instance, the words of one faculty member seemed to reflect the sentiments of both faculty and students. He told us, "The president is a very aggressive person, highly respected by everyone. He's barging ahead, trying to make this a first-rate university. This bothers some people, of course, but on the whole most of us realize that the institution has to be pulled up by its bootstraps. As long as we all feel that we can go to talk with him, to ask him questions if need be, most of us are content to have him push along. I think this idea of being able to identify ourselves with the president is highly important. As a result, the whole attitude around here seems to be one of mutual respect, even considering the different age and capacity levels." At another college, however, several students mentioned, "I saw the president when he spoke during freshman orientation. I'll probably see him next month at commencement, too, if he doesn't have something more important to do."

The occasionally or regularly scheduled meeting of student leaders with faculty members and administrative officers for discussion of common problems has been mentioned previously but bears repeating. We found it a most effective means in maintaining adequate communication. On many campuses, devices such as this have supplanted the time-honored convocations or chapels, which have given way to the pressures of increased enrollment as well as more complicated daily schedules. Despite its size, however, Brigham Young University continues a weekly assembly designed to keep students informed of the thinking of faculty and church leaders. It is voluntarily attended regularly by over half the students. Some colleges issue daily bulletins with pertinent information, although these seldom transmit items of policy.

We found, too, that the feeling of belonging and participating was strengthened by a continuing attempt to interpret the role of the college. It was surprising to us to observe the number of students who appeared to go through an institution without ever knowing what it was they just went through. Some faculty members expressed to us genuine concern that the student who fails to appreciate the free university in action may also fail to appreciate the free society. As one expressed it, "He will have missed an opportunity to sense the dependence of the national life on its instruments of education." A professor of mathematics added, "The college shouldn't hesitate to make known at every opportunity just why it exists. There are principles illustrated here which can be of tremendous importance in the attitude of a citizen ten or twenty years from now:" And a student exclaimed, "I wish I really knew what education is all about. The president gives speeches all over the country. He describes higher education to everybody but those of us who are being educated." We believe that college administrators and faculty members may help in many ways to interpret education. The president of Macalester College, for instance, has been writing a weekly column in the student newspaper, reflecting his views on many different subjects. He told us that he looks upon this as one of his major responsibilities.

There appeared to be increasing interest on a majority of campuses in discussions of educational means and ends. At the University of Colorado, for instance, we received enthusiastic reports of a series of lectures on education entitled "The Endless Search." We were told that a special series on "The Goals of Education" at another institution, Swarthmore College, was one of the highlights of the year. Informed, able, and intelligent speakers addressed large audiences of students and faculty members. Several colleges were also attempting to bring to the campus as lecturers men and women who were graphic examples of those who contribute substantially to the general welfare by their thinking. At one state university, through the annual fund drive, the alumni support a distinguished lecturer-in-residence for one term of each year.

Whatever the method, we believe that the potential of environment is measurably increased by a feeling of community. And that feeling appears to begin where it should—in common understanding and acceptance of commonly shared ideas and goals.

Personal Relationships on the Campus

We noted also that the level of interpersonal relationships was important as a contributing factor in the environment. The opportunity these relationships provide for effective communication on a campus has far-reaching results.

FACULTY TO STUDENT

We found that free student contacts with faculty frequently helped substantially to counteract the strong influences of exclusively student groups. Where faculty members became an important part in the students' lives, students modified their initial and often antagonistic reactions about adults, reactions which had grown into their thinking from early youth. As one student put it, "When we get to know some of these faculty members, we discover it isn't so bad to get old!" We were discouraged to note, however, that on some campuses students had only the most superficial acquaintance with faculty members. At one institution, for instance, five students mentioned that, as seniors, they knew no faculty member well enough to ask for personal references for jobs or graduate study. This may be the fault partly of the individual student but certainly not entirely.

Unfortunately on many campuses, both large and small, we observed that faculty contact beyond the classroom was often limited to pleasant social interruptions in the daily educational schedule. Faculty members poured and sipped at teas as well as chaperoned parties, but they resisted the student interest in opportunity for genuine give-and-take beyond the curricular structure. Perhaps teachers who now cringe at informal relationships with students because it robs them of time which could be devoted to scholarship might hold a different view were those relationships more respectable intellectually—in other words, were the faculty member actually put on his nettle by the inquiring mind of the student.

The relationship with the faculty member does begin in the classroom, but, we believe, it need not stop there. Occasionally students complained that some of their teachers selected their office hours solely at their own convenience without any thought of the availability of students. We noted, for instance, that one faculty member posted his available hours as Monday, Wednesday, and Friday at 11 A.M., the one hour when the majority of students were attending classes.

As there is a trend to pay students to undertake responsibility, apparently on some campuses there is also a trend in the feeling of some faculty that their informal contacts with students should be subsidized. For example, several faculty members mentioned to us that they would be happy to entertain students if funds were available. We were impressed not only by this unique method of rationalization but by the low priority which these faculty members gave student contact. We are led to observe that sometimes students like to talk as well as eat. In speaking of his professor one student commented, "I get the feeling that he's a good Joe because he's paid to be a good Joe. He really doesn't like the role."

At Wesleyan University the attempt has been made to encourage faculty members to relate themselves more directly to individual fraternity units. Each fraternity selects one or two faculty members and extends to them an invitation to eat luncheon at the house throughout the course of the year. Faculty so invited usually eat two or three lunches a week in the fraternity. In this way both students and faculty members have an informal opportunity on a continuing basis to understand each other, a basis far different from the superficial relationship frequently found.

An additional point emerging from our observations was that, to be effective and productive, faculty-student relations should not be overly structured. Spontaneity and informality marked many of the more successful relationships which we observed. Students told us also that the faculty members who "really mean something to us seem to be the ones who just plain like young people. If they begrudge the time they give us, we'd prefer to let them cross back over their moats and hide in their ivory towers." Students emphasized also the importance in the faculty member of a lively sense of humor which contributes to a perspective on the self. As one student commented, "It's rather hard to describe, but if he can laugh at himself, we really don't mind his laughing at us." Above all, students seemed to resent self-righteousness in the faculty member who expects the student to respect him and bow to him, especially if this means automatic acceptance of the faculty member's beliefs and standards.

We found, too, that the faculty can contribute to breaking the lock-step of student conformity. They extricate the student from the pervasive peer influence. But if it is only a hit-and-miss operation, the student will, of course, fall back into the peer group as soon as the faculty member ceases his contact. We might add also that we heard many faculty members confess that their contacts with students proved a stimulus to a re-evaluation of their own reactions and attitudes.

On the campuses which we visited we observed highly mixed reactions to the idea of faculty members entertaining students in their homes. The success of the activity appeared to depend heavily on the total attitude toward all faculty-student relationships. At Stetson University, for instance, we found faculty "firesides" to be informal in nature and strong in influence. The most graphic example was the weekly discussion held in the home of the dean of liberal arts. For many years the dean and his wife have opened their home each Tuesday evening to all interested students. Some years ago, on student request, this became a year-round activity.

The dean has established simple rules of precedure: All would be welcome and all, faculty members and students alike, would carry equal influence and prestige during that particular evening. The topics would be only those which the participants wanted to discuss. Although the discussions would not be confidential in one sense, particular points of views should never be quoted or identified outside of the group. Students told us that the rules helped to establish rapport and permitted freedom to express opinions without consequence.

The dean's fireside defies any concrete evaluation, but we found many students who attested to its value for them. We noted that it was one of the most cohesive elements on the campus leading to mutual respect and interest among faculty members and students. The dean told us, "I never let anything stand in the way of Tuesday night, even though it sometimes cuts down my participation in community activities. It think it deserves this importance." A Stetson student told us that for him "the firesides have been contagious. I want very much to do the same for others sometime. It's sort of a bug with me. I've changed from a business major to teaching as a result. I've entered the Honors Program, and now I'm going to have a Woodrow Wilson Fellowship next year."

The United States Naval Academy has recognized recently the importance of the informal contact. The superintendent of the Academy has established a Plebe Sponsor Program in which all faculty members and administrative officers of the Academy who want to participate are invited to sponsor one or more first-year students. The sponsors are expected to open their homes to the plebes and occasionally to invite them to dinner. They attempt to assist in solving personal and social problems. This appears especially important in the more impersonal and rigid disciplinary setting of the Academy. The program gives the plebes the opportunity, not otherwise provided, to become better acquainted with civilian faculty members as well as career officers. Particularly in the important first year, it helps make the Academy less austere and forbidding.

STUDENT TO STUDENT

We found evidence to suggest that, particularly in the residential college, the student has a profound effect on his fellow students—in fact, so profound that the college should be concerned with providing the right opportunity for the right effect. We believe that with proper attention the college can benefit from the education of students by students. The student is a person who acts and reacts like anyone else. We noted, for instance, that when he finds himself in need of assistance of any sort, he naturally turns first to his fellows. This was especially obvious on campuses where there was an absence of free communication with members of the faculty. The student knows that his fellow students can be counted on to understand his problems because they are facing many of the same problems and are making the same decisions.

We found that the right sort of informal education of student by student has many advantages. We observed, for example, the free exchange of ideas among students without fear of ridicule or condemnation. Here the student was able to test his ideas outside of the adult orientation. He had the opportunity to try himself out in relation to others of his own age and interests. So tested, we noted that he appeared to gain in self-understanding. In many cases, he might discover that his hopes and fears were more universal than he realized, that others of the same age can face and have faced similar problems without despair, that the clear thinking and determination they exhibited could be possible in his life, too. For an illustration let us turn to one freshman with whom we talked. He told us that he was having great difficulty with his parents. When he came to college, he thought he would be free of their minute supervision. But when vacation arrived, he discovered that his mother and father directed practically everything he did. That evening this same student participated in a dormitory bull session in which the subject of parents came up. When others began to discuss their parental difficulties, all of which were similar to his, a look of obvious relief came over his face.

Whether the college likes to admit it or not, we found that one of its major contributions to the student is in providing him with the opportunity to acquire the ability to get along with people whose backgrounds and interests are dissimilar. We observed, however, that the implications of this adjustment are not quite so social and anti-intellectual as some might fear. "Getting along" often included the ability to adjust intellectually through enlarged knowledge as well as to discover that apparently sincere people can honestly hold different positions. On campuses with large classes, often the out-of-class life was the only arena for such adjustment. The presence of foreign students on a campus encouraged this kind of give-and-take, although we noted that, in at least several colleges, foreign students were excluded from the usual kind of bull sessions and informal discussions. A reticence on the part of both foreign students and American students prevented effective assimilation. As a result, the students from other lands were apt to form their own group and remain out of the usual formal and informal student activities.

Like all human beings, the student is not without a need of security, a feeling of the sense of belonging. His entire outlook and attitude may change, we conclude, and he may become far more receptive to the processes and possibilities of education if the environment provides the opportunity to gain respect *for* others as well as the respect *of* others.

We are of the strong opinion that the relationship between the sexes is an important element in the environment. The attitudes of men students toward women and the women toward men sometimes can either encourage or negate much of what happens on a campus. We reach this conclusion after visiting several campuses where the relations were anything but normal. We found, for instance, serious unhappiness and unrest in colleges where members of a single sex were enrolled and where there was little opportunity for mingling with the opposite sex. At one college for men a student told us, "The lack of girls around here is a strangely disturbing factor. The guys have nothing to do so they go drinking. They live for the week ends when they can ride off in their cars to a women's college." And, from their table conversations and small talk in the dormitories and fraternities, we agreed that many of the students did seem to live for the week ends.

We should not give the impression that this happens only in the colleges enrolling just men or women. In our travels we came upon an interesting circumstance which indicated that it does happen elsewhere. Our two staff observers visited one campus at the same time. One lived in a women's dormitory and the other in a dormitory for men. They spent their time with the students and arranged to get together once or twice daily to compare notes. Their reactions to campus life kept conflicting. At the end of the visit we were faced with two completely different impressions of the same institution. On analysis, we discovered that the attitude of the women students in that college was quite different from that of the men. The men were enthusiastically involved for the most part; the women often were bitter and cynical. Further exploration led us to conclude that the social life, or the absence of social life, for the women conditioned substantially the attitude they held toward everything else that happened to them. When we attempted to get the women to discuss their courses and their teachers, for instance, they returned the conversation frequently to the "poor quality" of the boys on campus, to the male-female ratio, and to the absence of dates. There was apparent an underlying bitterness which was leading to a breakdown in morale and a general dissatisfaction over the entire collegiate experience. College officials, aware of this condition, confirmed our impression. Attempts were being started to alleviate a potentially troublesome and certainly discouraging situation.

We found that in all colleges a constructive social life was an important part of the environmental influence. Following the right kind and amount of relaxation, students appeared to return to the job of being students refreshed and invigorated. In such a climate, social activities were not regarded as an escape from or reaction against the real business of college life, but rather as recreation in the literal sense of the word.

Again, in some circumstances, we found that faculty members and administrative officers were judging the students by their own past experiences and attitudes. We discovered, for instance, that a number of faculty members failed to appreciate that the student today is likely to be more sophisticated. A new experience in colleges twenty years ago is probably "old stuff" to the student today. On one campus several faculty members quoted to us the words of a recently retired professor of philosophy who remarked, "When I first began teaching, practically everything I said shocked my students. Then came the time when nothing could make them move a muscle. Now I'm in the most distressing phase of all—everything they say shocks the life out of me."

The social life on many campuses was, we found, obviously influenced by an overdependence on synthetic stimulation from alcoholic beverages. This, of course, is a cultural problem and one not confined by any means to the colleges and their students. The campus is only reflecting fundamental changes in the social pattern. We observed, for example, that the dependence on drinking had the effect of deadening the use of imagination and precluding creativity in the planning of social activities. Students remarked that they were involuntarily supporting a social emphasis which ridiculed planned parties. "To have a party around here, all you do is get a keg and invite people," several agreed. And then they added, "We'd like to do something else besides drink, but we're not going to be the first ones to suggest it." If the college can solve this problem, we conclude, obviously it will contribute to the student's ability to live constructively in a society which is increasingly dependent on alcohol in its social life.

The wise and constructive use of leisure time is an integral part of the full use of one's faculties. We listened to one vice-president who told a student group, "Too many students try to be Paul Revere all night and Rip Van Winkle all day. It's unfashionable to take care of yourself."

Where the Student Lives

In the residential college the student spends a large share of his time in the more limited environment of his living quarters. We believe that living units can be of substantial benefit not only to the individual student but to the entire campus. Generally speaking, we would conclude that colleges have failed to realize the potentiality of the living unit both in supplementing the academic program and in contributing to the character of the student.

We noted that the living unit supplies a sense of belonging, particularly in the large college and university. If the campus is permeated with the shared conviction about which we have been speaking, then the belonging becomes more than membership in a dormitory or fraternity; it becomes membership in the learning community. If, however, life in the living unit is regarded as an escape from the intellectual community, then the living unit becomes a drag on the first purpose of the college. For example, we watched with interest the furor on one campus because a fraternity brought the Playgirl of the Month to the campus for a weekend party. *"This,"* one professor exclaimed, "is not what I consider appropriate!"

Our experience of living in all types and sizes of dormitories, fraternities, and sororities across the country convinces us that much of what happens in the living unit depends on the quality and philosophy of the adult leadership. We refer to the personnel deans, dormitory managers, individual house directors, and counselors. We came across many who had a deep concern for students and for their common life together. We met others, however, who appeared to view the management of the living unit as a holding operation. The students soon recognized this approach. The president of a dormitory told us, "Around here, responsibility is just a neat way of saying the college doesn't want to get caught allowing something embarrassing to happen." And a dean was frank enough to add, "We talk about rules as a device for teaching responsibility. Actually they are a convenient way of making sure we know what's going on."

On some campuses we noted what we would regard as an oversensitivity to the expectations of the public, notably the parents of the students. We conclude that if the college attempts to conform to all these expectations, the student will soon become a limp, docile kind of vegetable without energy or enthusiasm. Too often students are criticized as if they were somehow a breed apart, something to be judged by entirely different standards. On the one hand, they are accused of having no spark, and, on the other hand, heads shake when the spark ignites occasionally in the wrong way. Some appear to forget that youth is a time of ferment, not cement.

We found frequent instances in which the living unit served important purposes in the lives of students. An editorial in a student newspaper commented on the advantages to the new freshmen:

Since the advent of deferred (fraternity) rushing, dormitory counseling has assumed a greater importance than ever before. The freshman now has at least a full term before he is lavishly treated to the advice of fraternal big brotherhood and the stabilizing influence of fraternity mores in general. An upperclassman in his dormitory corridor, willing to help him with various social and academic problems whenever they arise, is in a position to do a lot in helping the freshman start his college career in the right manner, though many counselors have since regretted the remark they made at the beginning of the year, "Come on and knock at my door any time, boys, even at 4 A.M."

Denison University emphasizes joint student-faculty responsibility for educational policy. It carries this emphasis into the dormitory system, perhaps best illustrated by the dormitories for women originally called Honor Dorms. As with any innovation, student administration of dormitories came after a long period of education and experimentation. It has now progressed to the point where only the freshman dormitories have resident adult supervision. All upper-class units are governed by student officers and house councils, with each girl honor-bound to observe regulations and report infractions. In addition, there is a full-time residence counselor who acts in an advisory capacity to all dormitories and is on call to each living unit.

We observed several interesting results from the Denison system. University officials and students alike reported that rule-breaking is negligible, and, in fact, the girls have a feeling of responsibility rather than a "beat the system" attitude. We were told that parents, often the alleged reason for heavily regulated living units, accept the program enthusiastically after it has been explained.

FORM AND FUNCTION IN THE DORMITORY

We noted, too, that the actual design and functioning of dormitories and houses are often keys to what takes place within the structure. The three-story, small hotel which characterizes many dormitories is being subjected to scrutiny and, in some cases, to radical change on a number of campuses. Long hallways of rooms, relieved only by the occasional "common room," are recognized as inadequate. We were told and we found for ourselves that they breed the kind of impersonality which lessens the possibility of a "mode of association." Potentially, we believe, the hotel-type dormitory has much less chance of contributing to the intellectual life of the student. Occasionally we did find an honest attempt to surround the student with the tools of the mind in this setting. Several colleges were experimenting with the provision of a new type of dormitory library—a varied collection of the best of paperback books available to the student who wants to spend a few minutes or a few hours expanding his reading beyond the minimum assigned in course work. One dormitory set up a small bookshelf next to the telephone, knowing that students often wait there to complete a call. Several dormitories engaging in this experiment reported that, rather than books being stolen or taken away by mistake, the collection had been increased by students who brought their own volumes down from their rooms so that others might read them.

Experiments with design are under way on a number of campuses. Wesleyan University, for instance, recently has constructed new freshman dormitories limited in capacity to eighteen students with one counselor. The university hopes to make the living experience more personal and more productive. We noted an imaginative innovation in the Heritage Halls at Brigham Young University. The halls consist of sets of apartments, each accommodating six women students who do their own cooking and housekeeping, an arrangement that produces a measure of independence as well as a more homelike atmosphere. At Cornell University plans have been drawn for a residence center for law students contiguous to the law school's academic building. The *Cornell Daily Sun* editorialized:

> The idea of a residence center, not merely a dormitory, is particularly significant, since this could mean the start of a trend at the University. . . . Furthermore the center's inception comes at a time when there is considerable feeling that some of the University's living units, such as the men's dormitories, were constructed in such a manner as to accentuate rather than alleviate the anti-intellectualism that seems all too prevalent. . . . These dormitories have the effect of driving the students away from what could and should be one of the essential parts of the educational experience—the living units.

We found that experiments in function were also widespread. The cooperative dormitory or house is in operation at such institutions as Wisconsin, Arizona, Denison, Oberlin, and Radcliffe. We believe that they are excellent testimony again to the ability of the student to maintain full-scale domestic responsibilities while carrying on academic work. More important than any culinary skills which might be learned in the line of duty, we observed the *esprit de corps* which seemed to mount as students worked together. Administrators on several of these campuses reported to us that there was a significantly higher level of achievement among students living in cooperatives as compared with their neighbors in the traditional dormitories.

Regardless of the form of the particular housing unit, it is important for the student to have some opportunity for quiet, uninterrupted study. Students repeated this to us over and over again. But we observed also that the opportunity depends in large measure on the attitude within the living unit, not just on the structure itself.

STRENGTHS AND WEAKNESSES IN THE FRATERNITY

In some form or another, the fraternity system was a part of slightly more than half the campuses which we visited. In almost all cases our observers lived part of the time in the fraternities or sororities; in the few instances where they did not, they ate lunches or dinners there and spent afternoons and evenings conversing with the members. Out of this experience we conclude that few, if any, of the colleges have realized the full potentiality of the fraternity system. In some cases (more often than not), we felt that these units, despite their possibilities, had become a drag on the educational process. This seemed less true, we might add, with sororities. In the colleges which we visited, not all students, by any means, were members of fraternities or sororities, but on each campus where they were strong, we noted that all students were affected either directly or indirectly by their presence.

We were forced to conclude that fraternities at their worst had become islands of anti-intellectualism with the waves of true learning only lapping at the shores. It was difficult at one fraternity, for instance, to find students with whom to converse; the feature movie on television drew rapt attention night after night. In some cases we found that the fraternities did in fact dictate student aims. The results of rushing, for instance, appeared to us to determine in large part the kind and quality of an individual student's education.

We soon found that individual members were quick to acknowledge the shortcomings but slow to attempt reform. One institution reported, for instance, that a proposal to have an educational director in each house in order to promote scholarship had caused no small stir. Perhaps the relatively brief period spent on campus accounts for some of the student indifference and reticence toward change.

It seemed to us that the fraternity too often lost sight of the value and dignity of the individual member. One brother commented, "The fraternity swallows us up—and our values, too. Only the boys with really strong convictions hold out. They're respected but they are still individuals, not really a part of the house." In an editorial a campus newspaper concluded,

Now all of this is not to say that a thoughtful student or a conscientious and ardent worker cannot be a member of a fraternity. He can be; he is. But he must remember at all times that the attitude of his confreres is different from his, and that when he refuses to go drinking on a Friday night, he may be branded a grind, or a turkey, or whatever the current fraternity phrase is. He may be successful in his acceptance of the subtle criticism, he may not end up an outcast—but he is always aware that the disapprobation exists.

A fraternity member told us, "Our house is okay, I guess, but I really wish I'd joined in my junior year after I'd first had the chance to find out who I am and what I am. . . ."

In many of the groups which we visited, the "togetherness" theme was so paramount that it resulted in a one-sided emphasis on what the individual could do for the group, rather than what the group might contribute to the individual. Obviously this kind of approach contributed substantially to a group conformity. A sorority member reported, "I have a real gripe with my sorority sisters when they attend fraternity parties. They always complain about not having a good time and how immature the fraternity men are. Yet, in the presence of their dates, they act the same way. There is so much sameness and superficiality in their behavior and conversation."

We noted on some campuses that the fraternity obviously and traditionally chose for membership a certain "type of man" which, from our observations, served only to limit rather than to broaden the student's opportunity to understand his fellow students. In addition, the fraternity usually made heavy demands upon the student's time and loyalties, thus further limiting the possibility of his outside contact with other students. It was not uncommon for allegiance to the particular house to be stressed over allegiance to the college. Often the matter was trivial but the principle appeared to be important, at least to the administrator. As one told us, "Every year we try to get fraternity men to help with Homecoming, but every year we find they're too busy working on their own decorations and plans." More serious examples were reported, of course, such as the priority given a compulsory fraternity picnic over an all-campus honors convocation which recognized academic achievement.

We cannot help but conclude that the fraternity system is a strange anomaly on some college campuses. In many ways it is so close to what the college so often seeks in a dormitory system—relatively small in size, closely knit, and a unit of total education with special responsibility for campus leadership. It offers the opportunity for an unusual maturing process with group idealism balanced by individually held values. In many ways, too, it offers the student the right kind of security. As a student columnist wrote,

What is to be said for the fraternities? Well, there is the undeniable point that they provide a kind of social center for a group of men. It may be only a weekend party; it may be only the opportunity to relax in reasonably comfortable surroundings; it may be only camaraderie among a few special friends. But each of these is important, and to many people this can mean a lot. When one is uprooted from home life, there is a kind of security in knowing that some of the home life can be recaptured within a fraternity.

And, we would add, where student needs are met, the student should be expected to devote himself with greater vigor to the intellectual task.

This is what the fraternity could be. It has each of these important potentials—important not just to the membership but to the college of which it should be an integral part. But this is not what was reported to us or what we found, except in several isolated but encouraging cases.

We observed something further, however. From our study we concluded that today's fraternity system, as viewed by its members, was catering to far different needs and interests from those of the fraternity of previous generations. We detected a drifting away from "the glory of old Tri Phi" and from strict allegiance to and dependence on "the national." We felt that the interests of the local chapter were receiving increased emphasis, partly because the national society was considered to be insensitive to the present-day student. Another columnist commented, "Perhaps the greatest deterrent to modern thinking in fraternity affairs is the older member who, forty years after his graduation, is still trying to run the organization the way it was done while he attended college. These men usually have the fraternity's interest at heart, but their acts may well be the cause of an eventual breakdown of the fraternity system."

We do not agree that this may cause the breakdown of the system, but we do conclude that the combination of localism with the traditional potentialities of the small group unit might well provide fertile ground for revitalizing the fraternity contribution to campus life. Especially on the larger campus, these relatively small and homogeneous units could be much more than social whirlpools. There are indications of a growing sense of their possibilities. We found that many groups have been adopting the practice of inviting faculty members to participate regularly in discussions—not the occasional one-shot performance but an informal series on a formally established schedule. Some chapters which we visited had scholarship officers with responsibility for the educational program in an effort to offset the heavy emphasis on the social. These officers had made provisions for study rooms and study tables and for the tutoring by the more experienced of those in academic difficulty. Members were donating funds for house libraries in order to have something to put on the shelf next to the 1912 edition of an encyclopedia donated by an alumnus who was cleaning out his attic. A few were making a conscious effort to find house mothers with training in counseling and group work.

On several campuses we observed the beginnings of a potentially strong interfraternity government group. On several others the groups had already become active and responsible units. At the University of Arizona, for example, the twenty-four social fraternities are organized into an Interfraternity Council which is patterned after the system of checks and balances in the Federal Government. The Arizona IFC is divided into three branches: a committee of elected major officers constituting the executive branch; the judicial committee headed by the vice-president of the council and composed of elected representatives making up the "supreme court"; and the council itself as the legislative body. The council meets biweekly to discuss and establish major policy.

The Arizona IFC sponsors and directs such activities and service projects as rushing, alumni and pledge councils, intramural sports, scholarship programs, orphan parties, fire inspection of houses, group insurance plans, the March of Dimes and Crusade for Freedom campaigns, guide service for the campus, Help Week in place of the old Hell Week, the "Apple Polishers" dinner to acquaint faculty members with fraternity activities, and Greek Week which includes, in addition to social and athletic events, exchange dinners with other fraternities and sororities, and all-campus convocations featuring nationally known speakers.

Though its organization and program are perhaps no different from those of other councils on other campuses, we noted at Arizona an unusually positive spirit among the members as well as strong support from the administrative officers of the university. Whenever a group is needed for some unexpected job, or whenever youthful enthusiasm borders on campus vandalism, the council acts quickly and efficiently to remedy the situation. Its influence appears to spread to, but not to dominate, other campus bodies. Fraternity men, for instance, play an important part in the Student Representative Council. At Arizona the presidency of the IFC is one of the most cherished of campus offices. The high reputation of the council is a result, we believe, of a continuing student leadership which is above average in quality, of the close cooperation with the faculty and administration, and of successful attempts to carry on activities which transcend the usual housekeeping functions of such organizations.

This influence is subtle—difficult to describe or measure—but we believe that, in practice, it makes the difference between a threatening social group and a cooperative organization striving to combine the fun of college life with constructive programs.

At Wesleyan University an attempt is made to emphasize individual responsibility for fraternity affairs. It reaches its highest point in the Board of House Presidents, a body consisting of the presidents of each of the fraternities. The board operates under a code which defines in general terms the conduct expected of Wesleyan students. Through the board, each fraternity president, together with his fellow house officers, assumes responsibility for any infraction of the code. Further than this, they are held directly responsible for any trouble. If, for instance, an infraction does occur within a particular house, the president is personally responsible for taking steps to prevent a repetition. Thus the fraternity is expected to act on its own, but the board stands ready to step in if, in its opinion, the punitive and remedial action is not sufficient.

Wesleyan fraternities also engage in constructive programs to improve educational opportunities on the campus. On their own initiative several fraternities have sponsored series of lectures, forums, and concerts covering a wide variety of subjects and interests. Among the men brought to the campus by the fraternities in recent years have been Thornton Wilder, W. H. Auden, Malcolm Cowley, Saul Bellow, and Robert Penn Warren.

A fraternity at Cornell University with strong alumni support started recently a program designed to bring to the house three or four leading alumni for a long week end several times a year. The alumni live in the house, eat meals there, and are available for consultation and discussion. At least once during their visit, they address a general house meeting on the opportunities and responsibilities in the fields which they represent. The fraternity members thus are given the chance to talk in an informal setting with men in various professions, as well as to sense the general interest of alumni in both the individual members and the house as a unit. The alumni association of the fraternity pays the travel expenses of the visitors.

We noted with interest that on some campuses the sororities were taking the leadership and setting the example for the fraternities. Often what the sorority did and the way it did it stimulated the fraternity to expand its attention to more serious matters. One small example of a serious sorority activity came from the campus of the University of Colorado. The sorority gathered as a group to listen to the taped observations of an Army psychiatrist reporting on the discouraging record of American prisoners of war in the Korean conflict. The report raised questions about the motives and beliefs of American youth. One sorority member told us that her house had discussed the subject late into the night and for several days following. The girls were particularly disturbed by the large number of American prisoners who capitulated in captivity without the resistance and the discipline exhibited by prisoners from other nations.

We believe that the cohesiveness in the fraternity and sorority group is an excellent beginning point for an effective, constructive program. The fraternity system is another example of a group process which can be used to advantage in the educational effort, rather than merely condemned and left to its own devices. Its devices are not always, of course, neutral or negative. And the potentiality is apparent. An editorial in the *Cornell Daily Sun* observed:

> We are concerned with the University as a whole and the many educational threads that go into its pattern. That the fraternity system is a major thread—and a major threat—in this pattern seems to be significant to us, and indeed crucial to the future of the University. If Cornell is to become a greater institution, a strong and flourishing center of the academic and the intellectual—and it must—then the fraternities will have to play a part.

This view, we conclude, would meet with agreement on many other campuses.

The Larger Community

In our campus visits we noted also that the environment which surrounded the student often promoted a healthy and live awareness of the larger, outside community. The campus can, of course, become too confined, too parochial in its concerns. But, as one faculty member observed, "If students are to play the expected role of community, national, and world leaders, the college should give plenty of opportunity for understanding and practicing the larger citizenship."

In some instances we found that student initiative often supplemented the planned efforts of the college in this respect. For example, a local chapter of the national senior women's honorary society Mortar Board assumed responsibility on one campus for a voting forum at the time of the last presidential election. The Mortar Board members felt that any encouragement to vote should stem from informed and intelligent understanding of the issues as well as the procedures involved. The forum provided basic information, including general as well as specific instruction on registration and voting procedures. Many students on the campus were eligible to vote for the first time. Some whose homes were too far from the campus were instructed in the use of absentee ballots. As part of the program, one representative from each party gave a short explanation of his party's platform for the coming election. Following this, a nonpartisan speaker commented briefly on the importance of voting and on ways of assessing candidates and platforms. The event, offered in cooperation with the local League of Women Voters, suggested not only the hows of voting but also impressed students with the need for intelligent participation in elections.

An interesting example of wide student participation in citizenship education occurs every four years at Oberlin College in the form of the campus presidential nominating convention. Since 1860, students have participated in this exciting, well-organized educational program. The chairman of the convention is elected in the spring prior to the convention and spends many weeks organizing the state delegations and selecting the chairmen for these delegations. From the beginning of the college year in the fall there is a continual series of forums presenting issues from both sides. Students debate about and then finally decide whether the convention in that particular year will be Republican, Democratic, or any other party which has support from any of the students. Various pressure groups are organized to represent such factions as labor, farmers, and industrialists. The state delegations hold meetings and study the attitudes and traditions of the states they represent. As one faculty member commented, "The activity involved is so intensive and of such duration that the faculty sometimes feel that academic affairs fight a losing battle during Mock Convention year."

National figures are invited to the campus to keynote the three-day convention and to chair the general sessions. The convention exposes the student to the practical politics of the national nominating sessions as well as creates great excitement and enthusiasm over the issues involved. Oberlin students struggle over such national problems as segregation and civil rights. The student delegates are placed in the interesting position of deciding whether they will adhere to Oberlin's traditionally liberal approach or adopt the sentiments of the state which they happen to represent.

The Over-all Climate of the Campus

In this chapter we have attempted to treat environment as the sum total of the experiences of the student while he holds membership in the college community. To what has been said here must, of course, be added the passages on the level of expectancy, teaching, curriculum, student responsibility, and religious opportunity. All of these make up the over-all climate. We have found, as we have indicated, that parts of the environment may be positive, some neutral, and some obviously negative. We believe it is within the control of the college which shall be which. And we believe further that the environment will never truly have a full impact on character growth until all of its components, large and small, important and relatively unimportant, reinforce the best which the college has to offer.

We like the words of Huston Smith in his volume *The Purposes of Higher Education:*

Any college worthy of the name will have a spiritual life of its own which makes of it more than an assemblage of teachers, students, and buildings. At best it will have an atmosphere which is felt to be different from other environments the moment one steps into it and which acts as a powerful developing force upon all who live within it. Such an atmosphere will be like mist in the sense that one cannot put one's finger on it, but no one should be able to stay in it long without becoming thoroughly soaked.[2]

[2] Huston Smith, *The Purposes of Higher Education* (New York: Harper & Bros., 1955), p. 189.

8. *The Selection of Goals*

IN THE PRECEDING six chapters we have attempted to identify and then to discuss and illustrate the elements on a campus which, we believe, can lead to the encouragement of excellence in intellect and character. Now that we have spoken of the potential, it would be well to turn our attention briefly to what the college asserts it will attempt to do. This we call the selection of goals. We think it highly important that the college make such a selection carefully and realistically lest it be open to charges of fraud and hypocrisy. It may set its aims high but those aims should be partially attainable; an honest effort at least reduces the severity of the indictment.

The Rationale for Character Education

For our part, we conclude that the college cannot escape a responsibility for character education. The college is a part of the culture, and the culture demands that judgments be made. There are those who contend that the college can and should be *completely* objective. We hold that this is an impossibility. The college can never be truly objective for the simple reason that inescapably it reflects and promotes the culture of which it is a part. In the selection of goals, therefore, we feel that it is better to admit honestly that the colleges are sometimes not what they pretend to be, and then to select goals which truly reflect the possible and the potential.

All of this, of course, is not to say that the college cannot be objective *within* the framework of the culture. This more limited objectivity is what we believe the college should attempt to achieve. If one wishes to argue against this stand and to take the position that the college can and must be *wholly* objective, then

166

we need only pose such a question as this: In any college, what would happen to the student or the faculty member were he unalterably opposed to the ideas and ideologies of the culture? If he were, for instance, violently antidemocratic and antireligious? The answer, of course, is that every college would reject him, some quickly and others in due time, but all eventually would do so.

Furthermore, the college holds to a basic value pattern integral to the culture. It encourages honesty, loyalty, courage, cleanliness, and hundreds of other "qualities" on which the culture at least tacitly places priority. The fact that a college faculty takes these so for granted demonstrates again the college's dependence on and reflection of the culture.

As we stated previously, the culture demands that judgments be made. It holds that the college student is a human being with responsibility for human acts. American society, for example, has recently awakened to the desirability of coupling the knowledge of the construction and operation of nuclear weapons with an understanding of the morality of their use. Technological advances thus have made the dual task of the college even more apparent.

There remain, of course, those who reject this view. They contend that institutional goals are too broad, too all-encompassing, that the college claims to do too much and fails in its attempt. Therefore, they hold, the college should limit itself to the promotion of but one competency, usually that of the intellect. The college should then be willing to stand or fall on its success or failure with this single objective. Such a position takes the view that the college has bowed too easily to the demands of its various publics, including notably the parents of the student who hope that their son may now develop in such a way as to offset the failures of his first eighteen years.

On the other hand, some educators, apparently puzzled by the fact that education is expected to do something of everything, insist upon highly complex goals. They fear the selection of more singular and particular objectives. If goals be complex, they hope that many different people—students and faculty members alike—will find their own aims expressed somewhere along the spectrum. This is the shotgun approach.

Still others are afraid to include development of character among the aims of the college because they conceive of it as something maudlin. They would rather trust that character develops without their attempting in any way to provide the opportunity. Some of them also rationalize that they can perceive no effect; therefore, why go to all this trouble? They do not recognize, perhaps, that four years may well be too brief a period for a growing youngster to sense honestly and fully what is happening to him. The student may not appreciate it because he is unaware of it. Certainly all of us, however, know of individuals who do not blossom until well after the usual flowering season. Is this, then we ask, a valid reason for not planting the garden?

KNOWLEDGE AND JUDGMENT

The essential purpose of the college is training for intelligent behavior. This includes the acquisition of knowledge *but* it also includes the ability to make relevant judgments and wise choices guided by the discipline of logical method. Here, we believe, is where the college initially may stress character education. The two purposes—enlarged knowledge and relevant judgments—are inseparable both in training and in practice. Education should be much more than the mere retention of subject matter. It should include the attitudes, habits, and allegiances which are part of an educated person because he has undergone the college experience. We may assume, however, that these are not the same attitudes, habits, and allegiances which the freshman brought with him to college. Hopefully, they have been altered, deepened, and intensified through the process of intelligent self-analysis leading not only to the comprehension of the self, but also to an understanding perception of all men and of the world in which they live. The responsibility of the educated man is that he make articulate to himself and to others what he is willing to bet his life on.

In the four years of continuing enlightenment, every course, every professor, every campus activity should make a contribution in its own fashion and degree to the examined life which now *is* worth human living. The result may be the beginning answer not merely to *Who is man?* but to *Who am I?* The educated student emerges with a sense of what it really means to be a human being.

We have maintained that character examination and modification occur within the whole pattern of experience on the campus. The subtle, less obvious influences, we believe, may have a stronger and more lasting imprint than the planned program. With this in mind, we hold that the college which seeks to encourage character must look to all phases of the collegiate experience—to the quality of its intellectual life as well as to the opportunity for experience through participation, to the examples it provides as well as to the total environment within which the examples operate. No one emphasis works its magic on every individual. What is important is that the college provide the kind of climate conducive to many opportunities and the maintenance of a moral tone which reinforces rather than negates the various possibilities.

VARIETIES IN APPROACHES

Each college approaches the dual task in its own manner. Those founded upon a religious orientation, and maintaining that commitment, consciously accept a bias. It is an institutional commitment to a tradition. The decision thus has been made; the individual may accept or reject it, but the commitment will not change. In many cases, of course, complete faculty acceptance and student adherence may not be insisted upon. The college may not, for example, inquire into the doctrinal assumptions of its new professor of mathematics. Nevertheless, the over-all goal does not change. It rests upon well-defined concepts regarding the origin, nature, and destiny of man.

The secular college has a different approach; its values are not derived from doctrine. The college has its roots, instead, in a society which is highly pluralistic. Such an institution prides itself on its freedom, but sometimes finds it difficult to define that freedom. The image of man, for example, is less clear, less systematic than that found in the church college. It is not so readily conceived and described. Nevertheless, the roots of the secular college are in the heritage of the past as well as in the vitality of the present. The college operates in the trust that the student, if he is at all attuned to his campus environment, cannot escape sensing where the college stands.

The college or university with many purposes must make its approach with special care. Frequently this is the institution upon which the greatest demands are made. Because it is attempting to do many things with large numbers, it must recognize that a special effort will be necessary to implement the goals it chooses.

METHODS FOR IMPLEMENTING THE GOALS

We believe that once the college has determined what it shall attempt to do, it has certain means within its control for achieving the result. We have stated, for instance, that it may establish its own level of expectancy, that it may choose faculty members with special criteria in mind, that it may provide the right conditions for effective teaching, that it may restructure its curriculum to add to the student's ability to judge as well as to his breadth of knowledge. Furthermore, the college may encourage participation by the student in his own education, and it may provide opportunity to profit from the religious heritage. All of the various facets of the environment contribute.

In addition, we believe that the college has the means to control to some extent the type and caliber of its student body. Once having established its reputation and made explicit its chosen goals, for example, the college will find that many of its students elect to enroll there because they know what to anticipate. If the college places its emphasis on individual needs, for example, it will probably draw to its campus many students desiring or feeling a need for individual attention. Or if it is a church-centered institution, it may expect to interest first the student who is concerned with religion. Similarly, the college exercises selectivity through its admissions policy. It may enroll only those who appear able to benefit from its special concern. There are, of course, conditions beyond the control of the college which reduce the chances of success in selecting students. We know too little about human beings to be able to determine exactly their particular strengths and weaknesses. The admissions policy thus may not always function properly. Furthermore, size enters into the picture. It is altogether conceivable that students may respond better to colleges of one size than another, regardless of the emphasis. Some students, for instance, benefit more from the cosmopolitan setting of the large university while others respond more quickly to the small college.

Barriers to Success

We must recognize also that other outside influences make more difficult the realization of the chosen aims. The student is subject to many practices and pressures originating off the campus but impinging on it. As we have concluded, this presents a special problem for the urban university. A different kind of problem affects the junior college in which students have a greater feeling of transiency. They recognize they are there either for a relatively brief terminal course or they are on their way to another institution.

Furthermore, the student does not arrive at the doorstep of any college as raw material might reach a factory. He is already shaped and stamped to some degree. The college receives what the home, the school, the church, and the community have thus far produced. In many ways, the early formative years provide the key to the limitations as well as the potentialities of the collegiate experience. Values are first discovered and developed in the arena of experience, and the college student is a product of eighteen years of experience. What takes place, therefore, is conditioned by what has preceded.

Neither the college nor the student is isolated from the social organization and pattern of which both are an integral part. The manners and morals of American society, as we have attempted to demonstrate, have been felt deeply in the colleges and by the students who are products of the society. The student brings with him to college both the strengths and the weaknesses of the pattern of life which has thus far surrounded him. The younger generation tends, for instance, to adopt without much hesitation the sham standards of our adult world which exalt material success.The student obviously changes his attitudes and his interests in terms of the changing power pattern in society. In the early colleges, for instance, many students studied theology because of the importance of the church in the society of their day. Present-day students gravitate in increasing numbers toward such a specialized field as business administration.

Perhaps in reaction against this strong influence, the student often regards his college days as a parenthesis in his life, between the brackets of which he can enjoy himself for the last time. For its part, the college attempts, on the one hand, to remove the brackets by encouraging the student to pursue vocational studies, while on the other hand it encourages him to look beyond the present and to seek the values which are greater than those found in the particular moment of history in which he lives. The more narrow and specialized the field of study, therefore, the more important it becomes to encourage students to confront value choices.

The question of goals raises also the question of the differences in education for men and for women. In the separate college for women, for instance, the goal is likely to include a broad, yet intellectually functional, training for women's place in society as *women*. There is a recognition that the responsibilities of women are different from those of men. In the coeducational college, for the most part, women students follow what has been established primarily for the men. Wherever they are, however, we find that women students are less inclined to view "the better self" as something achieved primarily through vocational fulfillment and materialistic enrichment. Overt idealism is not frowned upon. Generally speaking, the women want to be better and the men, better off.

With this in mind, the college which selects methods to implement its goals may discover that women students potentially are more receptive to direct character emphases than the men. Rarely did we find that male students in groups talked as openly and freely about their values and aims as did the women. This is a result partly of a simulated veneer of sophistication among men, and partly it is because, we believe, men cling more to the privatism which has developed from the Puritan ethic in American society. It was interesting to note that men felt more free to talk openly about values and aims when they were in mixed groups or with their dates.

The student's idea of education and what it should comprise is conditioned substantially by his own purpose in coming to college, which, in turn, has been affected by social demands. To us, the student appears to be a striking paradox, a strange mixture of the group conformist and the self-concerned individualist. He is a victim of temporary moods. One student, for example, told us, "I haven't felt any positive emotion in the last six months. Maybe I'm looking for something that isn't there." Two hours later, however, we observed this same student excited by and involved in a discussion on the answer to existentialism.

The student is drawn, too, by conflicting loyalties. He wants to shape his own life but also to contribute to the lives of others. Throughout his college days he maintains beneath the surface a buoyant optimism and a deep-seated faith that life is good. Furthermore, he believes it will hold for him all he wishes if he has the opportunity to shape it as he desires. This, to us, is the American optimist enrolled for higher learning. It is also, however, the American conformist ready to submit to the pressures around him.

Neither an Isolated Nor a Solitary Enterprise

These are some of the factors which the college must consider as it sets out to implement its stated aims. The college cannot operate in isolation; it must take into account the society around it and the competing allurements. The college accepts no small challenge if it decides that it will attempt to become a distinctive force in the life of the student. It must recognize, too, that the college student, by virtue of his four years on campus, will not become automatically the man of character. We do not expect his education to be completed; we should not, therefore, anticipate that character will be formed and made perfect in so brief a span of time. Instead, the college may provide the further impetus to a continuing self-education and self-energizing character formation. Education is not a solitary enterprise to which one gives a few years of his life; it is a continuing process, a slow and never-ending procurement of focus and direction. The contribution of the college is to force values out of abstract thought into consciousness where they may be re-examined and reaffirmed.

9. The Possible and the Potential

O UR ON-THE-SPOT study of students and faculty members in twenty colleges and universities has convinced us that presently there are untapped riches in both the colleges and the students. We have found much more about which to be encouraged than discouraged. There are major forces present on every campus which, if properly mobilized, can offer the student a truly distinctive educational experience.

In our study we have made a special effort to look closely at the framework within which the student gains his education and within which character change may possibly occur. We have observed what takes place in the classroom and the laboratory, in the dormitory and fraternity, in the meeting room and social center. We have talked with the instructor in English and the professor of physics, with the department chairman and the president, with the chaplain and the personnel dean. And we have talked with many students, the senior and the freshman, the leader and the led.

In observing the framework we were aware that much has been said of the diversity in American higher education. Our study, however, leads us to believe that there is much similarity among colleges and students across the nation. We encountered no substantial differences in basic attitudes from one college to another and from one region to another. We came across no major deviations in collegiate form and structure among types of institutions, as, for instance, the church-related college and the state university. What diversity there is, however, is not among the students or within the framework of the college. It is, we conclude, in the depth and the scope of the task which both the college and its students agree to pursue and in the intensity of the pursuit. No radical revision of the collegiate structure appears necessary but rather a careful re-examination of goals and practices.

Excellence in Intellect and Character

On every campus we visited we found a dedication to the pursuit of excellence in some form. But we noted also a great unevenness on every campus. In a particular situation, for instance, the student appeared to us to be enthusiastic and enthralled; in another circumstance, perhaps no more than five minutes later, he was dissatisfied and cynical. The challenge to the student exists now in various ways and through various means, but seldom does it permeate every campus endeavor. And seldom, therefore, we would add, does it really take hold within a majority of students.

We have attempted to examine the contribution which the college can make to consistent excellence in character as well as intellect. As a result, we have reached what to us is a major conclusion: that the college's unique and best contribution to character is a direct product of a properly balanced emphasis on learning. We found that the conditions conducive to the development of character are, in many ways, the same ones which are conducive to good teaching and sound learning. In similar fashion we would hold that the elements in the campus community which encourage character are those which also encourage learning.

We believe that the American college can achieve the dual goals of intellectual excellence and force of character. The two are inextricably interwoven in the truly educated man. The obligation of the college to strengthen and deepen the opportunity for this important dual dimension implies, not abandonment, but intensification of its primary purpose of intellectual development. We hold, therefore, that excellence of character in the educated man depends upon a more searching, more challenging, more strenuous collegiate experience in totality. The principles which call forth allegiance in the academic community are those which may also serve to guide the man of character in the world community.

THE SPECIAL ROLE OF THE COLLEGE

Each institution in our society, including notably the family and the church, makes a contribution to character enrichment. Supplementing these contributions, the college has a special role to play. Calling on the tools of the intellect, it lends analytical thought and perceptive examination to the values which have already been established. The college, we believe, finds its greatest contribution to the student in the Socratic theme that the unexamined life is not worth human living. The college can make possible this examination. Education then becomes more than mere enlargement of knowledge; it offers the potentiality of leading eventually to wisdom as the step beyond knowledge.

To our mind the student, beneath his façade of cynicism in strange combination with buoyant optimism, is ready to be challenged. This generation of college students may be silent at times and most loquacious at other times, "beat" one moment and out to beat the world the next, self-satisfied and frightened, but it is, by and large, aware of its growing pains and not particularly reticent about discussing them. If the stimulus is right, the student will respond. Without the right stimulus he will drift and finally moor in the haven which immediately appears most attractive.

THE BALANCED APPROACH

Obviously the development of character as well as intellect in the college is the result of no single influence or set of experiences. Our observations have led us to segregate six elements in particular. Two of them—the level of expectancy and the effect of environment—result from the over-all attitude and approach of the college. The other four—the concept of teaching, the organization of the curriculum, the degree of student responsibility, and the opportunity for religious understanding and practice—contribute to, as well as emerge from, all else that takes place. These six comprise, we believe, a yardstick against which the college might well measure its success in implementing its chosen goals.

At the present time one or more of these elements undoubtedly are the object of special emphasis on every campus. We conclude, however, that the most substantial modification of character cannot be achieved until the college actively promotes all six. In balance, the extent to which the college actually does affect a change in the attitudes and values of its students may well hinge on the degree to which it gives genuine support to this type of program. Though we believe that the college itself must balance its endeavor, we do not mean to imply that each student should be subjected to equal portions of all six elements. Fortunately human beings are not all alike: some students initially respond best to the stimulus of the teacher while others respond to the stimulus of the subject or of some phase of campus life. Our concern is that each student shall undergo an experience of excellence in at least some quarter early in his college career.

We have attempted also in this study to spell out some of the difficulties facing the college as it strives to develop character in its students. Though the difficulties are many, we are encouraged by the extent of intelligent concern and discussion we found among students and faculty members wherever we traveled. In addition, we have attempted to describe a few of the planned programs which further demonstrated that thoughtful consideration is translated into action on many campuses.

We have approached character as the commitment to principles. We have found that if the college seeks to encourage character development, it must place special emphasis on principles. In many ways, college life presents the last opportunity to challenge effectively and completely the assumptions of youth. Values may be brought out of the shadows of abstraction into the searching light of critical assessment. In this way, perhaps, they emerge as conscious guides. This is not the task of any one course or professor or particular phase of campus living. The total resources of the college should challenge the provincial thinking of the student. The greatest impact on character occurs as a result of the total campus experience, especially if the relationship between intellectual training and character is made a real one. One perplexing failure of the college, and one of its greatest challenges, is the development of critical, active, and inquisitive minds. This, we believe, is possible in vocational preparation as well as in liberal education. It is a matter of approach, of emphasis on principles, not a possibility limited to certain disciplines and fields of study.

The Need for Reappraisal

We believe that the college attempting to marshal its forces for this task must engage in a continuing reappraisal. We are concerned that the college at the present time takes itself and the assumed limits of its task too much for granted. It would be well, for instance, for every institution to ask itself: Who are these students with whom we deal? What do they want from us? What is this instrument we call the college? What do we want it to do? How is it best accomplished and what are the relative roles of students and faculty? What strengths does the college have to call upon? This study has, we hope, begun the identification of some of these strengths. We have noted, for instance, the honest urge on the part of the student for self-discovery, for a meaning to his existence. We have talked of his readiness, under the right conditions, to assume responsibility for his own education. We have mentioned his perceptiveness in sensing what is good teaching and what means the most to him in what he studies. We have discussed his relationship with his teachers and have implied the possibility of greatly improved communication and understanding. We have touched upon his interest in others, in what makes for similarities and what makes for differences in human beings.

Out of this study we conclude further that, if the college is to seek a larger role in the lives of its students, it is obligated to make a greater effort to break from tradition in both form and substance. It has been discouraging to us to see, for instance, how often the present rigidity of the college reduces its potentialities. Further experimentation obviously is desirable. We feel this so strongly that we take perhaps the unusual position that we need less attention henceforth to studies of the student and much greater attention to positive efforts to meet his needs. Studies of this kind can go on interminably but they have no value, beyond casual interest, until the colleges themselves attempt the new and the constructive. For example, since so much depends upon the environment which surrounds the student, the college should experiment with radical changes in the type and size of living units as well as with more imaginative programs eliciting the best from fraternities and sororities. Further experimentation is needed also in almost every other facet of the college program. Dissatisfaction with the marking and credit system, for instance, will never be mitigated until something better emerges out of a number of trials and errors. More could be accomplished by new approaches to teaching responsibilities and to the curriculum in which depth and breadth must be balanced. A new type of religious program might reach the student who is vaguely and hesitantly seeking as well as the student who is already interested and committed. Conceivably, the student could be convinced that morals are more than an individual, personal concern, and that, if he is to live effectively with others, he must take cognizance of man's mutual interdependence.

We trust that the entire study has pointed up other areas deserving imaginative experimentation. Tradition should not be allowed to stand in the way of constructive change.

AREAS FOR EXPLORATION

As we have suggested, perhaps the time has come to call a halt to the depth exploration of the student. Instead, research staffs might face with courage (for it will be needed) the possibility of a closer look at the faculty. If, as our evidence seems to indicate, the faculty member plays such an important role in the development of the student, we need to know more about him. Where does he come from? Where is he heading? What are his motives, his attitudes, his values? If the student is silent, is it because the generation before him is even more quiet? Here is a project deserving serious study.

An attempt might be made also to compare the student with the nonstudent. Is there a difference in attitude and in values between those who are attending college and those who choose, for one reason or another, not to continue education beyond the high school? Until we are sure, we cannot genuinely claim any effect of higher education. It is conceivable that much of what we like to think the college accomplishes is really due to natural maturation.

It would be well, too, to inquire into the forces for character growth in the primary and secondary schools. The college student is a product of his past. We need to know more about this past.

We sense also the necessity for expanded efforts to promote articulation between the college and both the high school and the high school student. What does best prepare students for the college experience? We are aware that some are not ready for the new experience while to others college is a repeat performance of high school days. Certainly a more effective introduction to the idea of higher learning is desirable. No orientation program, however, can ever replace a careful and gradual preparation achieved long before the student actually enters the college environment. The college and the high school must work together more closely to avoid what has become a subject of strong student complaint— the overly repetitive experience both in terms of curriculum and extraclass life. If there is student apathy, we venture to conclude that it may be due in part to the natural boredom facing any human being who is expected to respond with enthusiasm to an old experience.

An Obligation and a Challenge

No matter what we wish the colleges might achieve, and no matter how ardently and devoutly they approach their task, there will be problems of unquestionable magnitude in the decade ahead. The task of the modern college will be enlarged by increasing national demands and by the substantial growth in the number of college-age youth seeking the collegiate experience. Continuing attention to quality is imperative, however. And this means not just the quality of the intellectual enterprise but of all that happens to the young man or woman who spends four important years of his life on a college campus. In *The Art of Teaching,* Gilbert Highet cautions us not to criticize or to dismiss too easily: "[The students] have no faults, except the very ones they are asking you [the teacher] to eradicate: ignorance, shallowness, and inexperience. . . . It will be useless . . . to wish that there were only two or three, or that they were all more mature. They will always be young, and there will always be lots of them."[1]

The nation places its hopes and, indeed, its future in the caliber of leadership which the colleges can provide. Our study convinces us that the American college must be concerned with both competence and conscience in order to meet its special responsibilities. The two are requisites for effective leadership. Allegiance to one without proper attention to the other may result in the half-educated man. We must not allow preoccupation with the mastery of subject matter to cloud our vision of what could and should happen to the student. We must, instead, recognize that the college has within its community the energizing and unifying forces which truly make education a distinctive and lasting experience.

The college is not just tacitly responsible for character but actually responsible with a realistic hope of fulfillment. Its concern for the student is inextricably bound into the best attempts of

[1] Highet, *The Art of Teaching* (New York: Alfred A. Knopf, 1954), pp. 27, 28.

the human mind and spirit to interpret and to realize the immense possibilities in man. Again the words of William Jewett Tucker ring more true today than when they were first spoken more than fifty years ago: "Be not content with the commonplace in character any more than with the commonplace in ambition or intellectual attainment. Do not expect that you will make any lasting or very strong impression on the world through intellectual power without the use of an equal amount of conscience and heart." For the college as well as its students, this is at once both an obligation and a magnificent challenge.

APPENDIX

Colleges and Universities Cooperating in the Study

Name	Location	Undergraduate Enrollment*	Control	Sex
University of Arizona	Tucson, Arizona	8,180	State	Coeducational
Brigham Young University	Provo, Utah	10,138	Church	Coeducational
Colgate University	Hamilton, New York	1,365	Nonsectarian	Men
University of Colorado	Boulder, Colorado	9,623	State	Coeducational
Cornell University	Ithaca, New York	8,404	Nonsectarian	Coeducational
Denison University	Granville, Ohio	1,342	Church	Coeducational
Goddard College	Plainfield, Vermont	94	Nonsectarian	Coeducational
University of Louisville	Louisville, Kentucky	6,496	Nonsectarian	Coeducational
Macalester College	St. Paul, Minnesota	1,373	Church	Coeducational
United States Naval Academy	Annapolis, Maryland	3,781	Federal	Men
University of New Hampshire	Durham, New Hampshire	3,177	State	Coeducational
University of Notre Dame	Notre Dame, Indiana	5,343	Church	Men
Oberlin College	Oberlin, Ohio	1,999	Nonsectarian	Coeducational
Pasadena City College	Pasadena, California	8,348	Municipal	Coeducational
Radcliffe College	Cambridge, Massachusetts	1,074	Nonsectarian	Women
Saint Mary's College	Notre Dame, Indiana	951	Church	Women
Stephens College	Columbia, Missouri	1,498	Nonsectarian	Women
Stetson University	DeLand, Florida	1,444	Church	Coeducational
Wesleyan University	Middletown, Connecticut	742	Nonsectarian	Men
University of Wisconsin	Madison, Wisconsin	13,144†	State	Coeducational

* 1957–58 figures furnished by the individual colleges.
† Madison campus only.

Selected Bibliography

Among the many treatises and studies which provided useful background material and helpful insights, the following were especially valuable:

BARZUN, JACQUES. *Teacher in America.* Boston: Little Brown & Co., 1945.

FARNSWORTH, DANA. *Mental Health in College and University.* Cambridge, Mass.: Harvard University Press, 1957.

HARVARD STUDENT COUNCIL. *Religion at Harvard.* Cambridge, Mass.: Harvard Student Council, 1956.

HAVIGHURST, ROBERT J., and TABA, HILDA. *Adolescent Character and Personality.* New York: John Wiley & Sons, Inc., 1949.

HIGHET, GILBERT. *The Art of Teaching.* New York: Alfred A. Knopf, 1954.

JACOB, PHILIP E. *Changing Values in College.* New York: Harper & Bros., 1957.

LIGON, ERNEST M. *Dimensions of Character.* New York: Macmillan Co., 1956.

LUNN, HARRY H., JR. *The Student's Role in College Policy-Making.* Washington: American Council on Education, 1957.

RIESMAN, DAVID. *Constraint and Variety in American Education.* Lincoln, Neb.: University of Nebraska Press, 1956.

SANFORD, NEVITT (ed.). *Journal of Social Issues,* Vol. XII, No. 4 (1956). [A special issue devoted to a progress report of the research study undertaken by the Mary Conover Mellon Foundation at Vassar College under the direction of Dr. Sanford.]

SMITH, HUSTON. *The Purposes of Higher Education.* New York: Harper & Bros., 1955.

TAYLOR, HAROLD (ed.). *Essays in Teaching.* New York: Harper & Bros., 1950.

TEAD, ORDWAY. *Character Building and Higher Education.* New York: Macmillan Co., 1953.

TOWNSEND, AGATHA. *College Freshmen Speak Out.* New York: Harper & Bros., 1956.

AMERICAN COUNCIL ON EDUCATION

ARTHUR S. ADAMS, *President*

The American Council on Education is a *council* of national educational associations; organizations having related interests; approved universities, colleges, teachers colleges, junior colleges, technological schools, and selected private secondary schools; state departments of education; city school systems and private school systems; selected educational departments of business and industrial companies; voluntary associations of higher education in the states; and large public libraries. It is a center of cooperation and coordination whose influence has been apparent in the shaping of American educational policies and the formation of educational practices during the past forty-one years.

L